SQUARE FOOT GARDENING

ANSWER BOOK

First published in 2012 by Cool Springs Press, an imprint of the Quayside Publishing Group, 400 First Avenue North, Suite 400, Minneapolis, MN 55401

Cool Springs Press titles are also available at discounts in bulk quantity for industrial or sales-promotional use. For details write to Special Sales Manager at Cool Springs Press, 400 North First Avenue, Suite 400, Minneapolis, MN 55401 USA.

To find out more about our books, visit us online at www.coolspringspress.com.

Library of Congress Cataloging-in-Publication Data

Bartholomew, Mel.
  Square foot gardening answer book : new information from the creator of square foot gardening — the revolutionary method used by 2 million thrilled followers / Mel Bartholomew.
     p. cm.
  Includes index.
  ISBN 978-1-59186-541-4
1. Square foot gardening. 2. Container gardening. 3. Vegetable gardening. 4. Small gardens. I. Title.

  SB453.B3826 2012
  635--dc23

2012037772

Printed in U.S.A.

10 9 8 7 6 5 4 3

Design: Mandy Kimlinger
Layout: Diana Boger
Illustrations: Melanie Powell
Cover photo © Marcus Harpur
Photos on pages 19, 43 by Paul Markert

ANSWER BOOK

NEW INFORMATION FROM THE CREATOR OF
SQUARE FOOT GARDENING — THE REVOLUTIONARY
METHOD USED BY **2 MILLION** THRILLED FOLLOWERS

Mel Bartholomew

COOL
SPRINGS
PRESS
Growing Successful Gardeners™

MINNEAPOLIS, MINNESOTA

DEDICATION

This book is dedicated to all of our wonderful Square Foot Gardening fans who might need some slight clarification on some of the finer points of SFG. There may even be some that didn't quite finish reading the book and want to jump right into some of the answers. This book will give them just the sort of details they're looking for.

ACKNOWLEDGMENTS

I'd also like to thank all of our Certified Instructors who helped set up this book with suggested questions that they received and who also had helpful hints on how detailed to make the answers. Happy Gardening to all those who read this book.   —Mel

CONTENTS

INTRODUCTION

I invented Square Foot Gardening back in 1976, and I've been spreading the word ever since. I've received letters from readers and gardeners all over the world, and I've taught more people about Square Foot Gardening than I can count. I figure that at one time or another, I've heard just about every question a person can ask about this revolutionary method of gardening.

When I sat down to write the *ALL NEW Square Foot Gardening* in 2007, I looked to answer the questions that I had encountered since my first book, *Square Foot Gardening*, was published in 1981. I developed Square Foot Gardening as a simple alternative to wasteful, labor-intensive and inefficient row gardening. The refinements in this new edition from Cool Springs Press made the method even simpler and more straightforward than ever.

But people still come up with questions, so I wrote this book to share the answers to those questions with everyone, and to help gardeners everywhere get the most out of their gardens: whether or not they are true Square Foot Gardens.

A QUICK BIT OF HISTORY

Questions never bother me; I think they're a healthy part of any process. In fact, quite a while ago now it was a question that started me thinking about gardening in a brand new way. That question was "Why?" In 1975, I formed a community garden as a retirement project and saw firsthand how wasteful, time-consuming, and laborious row gardening can be. Despite everyone's best intentions, and a large initial group of enthusiastic community gardeners, by the end of the season our community garden was an overgrown mess, and many of the gardeners had burned out and simply given up.

I'm an engineer by trade, so I love to solve problems. As I thought about what had gone wrong, I realized that the whole system of row gardening just didn't make sense to me. So I asked that most important question: "Why?" Why plant a whole packet of seeds all in a row, only to then spend a lot of time and effort "thinning" out the seedlings to 2, 4 or 6 inches apart? Why constantly weed all those 3-foot aisles? Why till and improve and fertilize all that garden area every single year only to pack it back down as you walk around working in your garden? And the most important one: "Why garden in rows spaced 3 feet apart anyway?" The answer I got in every case was, "Because that's the way we've always done it."

As you can imagine, that answer wasn't good enough for an inquisitive engineer like me. That's when I invented Square Foot Gardening. It worked like a dream in 1976, when I instituted it in our community garden. It worked so well, in fact, that it got a lot of attention from local news outlets and the general gardening community. Pretty soon, more and more people wanted to know about this newfangled way of growing vegetables and flowers. For every person I taught about SFG, there were 10 more who wanted to learn. I knew the method could revolutionize gardening, and would save gardeners a lot of time, effort, tools, space and water. And I knew it would work for gardeners across the country—regardless of where they lived or what the local climate was. At a point, it only made sense for me to write a book to reach all those people. So I did, and the original *Square Foot Gardening* was published in 1981.

That only fed the fire. PBS caught wind of what I was doing and asked if they could come by and film short segments about SFG, calling them *A Minute in Mel's Kitchen*. Those segments grew into a full-blown show that had a five-year run on PBS on every channel in the system, and then eventually, three more years on the Discovery Network and The Learning Channel.

When the show came to an end, I figured I'd go back into retirement and enjoy my own quiet little garden. Well, as they say, the best laid plans of mice and men! When the Utah Board of Education came knocking, hoping to institute SFG in schools as a way to teach children, I just couldn't resist. I set up the Square Foot Gardening Foundation and came up with a curriculum and a program we called "A Square Yard in the School Yard." The program took off and we eventually installed Square Foot Gardens in schools across the country.

The SFG Foundation kept me pretty busy, especially once we connected with the Utah State Board of Education and agreed to put an SFG in every grammar school in the state! That was quite a challenge, but it was also rewarding to see children everywhere learning through SFG. Little did I realize that it would be just the start of the Foundation's work.

The SFG Foundation has done a lot to bring the message to people across America, but I realized it could solve even bigger problems. That's why we branched out and started working with international humanitarian groups to spread the word overseas, with the method tailored to an international audience, and called "Square Metre Gardening." From the Serengeti Plains to the foothills of Nepal, small Square Metre Gardens are making inroads against poverty and hunger. People across the globe are learning how to grow more with less, how to feed their families well with limited natural resources, and how to improve their lives using Square Metre Gardening.

I'm pretty happy with the way things have gone, but engineers just love to tinker. In all that time that has passed since the first book was published, I've been refining the SFG method. At one point, I organized those refinements into 10 important new improvements that I wanted to share. So in 2007, the *ALL NEW Square Foot Gardening* was published. That book became the largest selling garden book in America and the popularity of SFG continues to grow.

And the questions continue to come in. So much has gone on with SFG that I felt it was time to write a comprehensive user's guide gardeners could turn to for the answers to any and all questions they might have about SFG. It's important to me that people learn all the benefits of the SFG method and get any help they need if things don't make sense at first. This book includes all of the most frequently asked questions about SFG—starting with the 10 most common questions at the end of this introduction.

It's all part of promoting the healthy, environmentally friendly and life-affirming message of SFG. I figure if we keep at it, we can cover the whole world in healthy, productive gardens . . . 1 square foot at a time! It's an organic, practical and commonsense method, and it's friendly to both the user and the environment.

THE 10 COMMANDMENTS OF SQUARE FOOT GARDENING

1. Thou shalt not waste space with a large row garden.
2. Thou shalt not use or dig up your existing soil.
3. Thou shalt not use a hoe, shovel, or rototiller.
4. Thou shalt not waste seeds by planting and then thinning.
5. Thou shalt not remove your "SFG grid."
6. Thou shalt not use any fertilizer, insecticides, or pesticides.
7. Thou shalt not plant more than you can harvest or take care of.
8. Thou shalt not waste water by hosing, sprinkling, or irrigating.
9. Thou shalt not fail to grow all your vine crops on a vertical support.
10. Thou shalt not fail to replant each square foot as it is harvested.

THE SFG FOUNDATION: MAKING A DIFFERENCE

Based in Eden, Utah, the Square Foot Gardening Foundation is a non-profit organization dedicated to eradicating world hunger by teaching people around the globe how to grow healthy food with limited resources and effort, while involving all family members in an enjoyable activity. The SFG foundation pursues this goal through a range of projects, including:

- Educational programs and curricula to teach students about gardening and nutrition as they participate in SFG in their schools.
- SFGs donated to local communities and organizations.
- Cooperative programs with non-governmental organizations (NGOs) overseas, which teach individuals and communities the Square Metre Gardening method, with the aim to eradicate hunger and poverty and increase independence.
- Training programs and materials for those looking to become certified SFG teachers.
- All the materials necessary to build your own SFG.

You can learn more about the Foundation, its mission and programs, purchase equipment, supplies, and educational materials, or even donate if you wish, on the Foundation's website at www.squarefootgardening.org. Also check out the SFG website at www.squarefootgardening.com, and my personal website at www.melbartholomew.com.

THE 10 MOST FREQUENTLY ASKED QUESTIONS ... ANSWERED!

1. Why would I want a Square Foot Garden instead of an old-fashioned row garden?

The real question is why WOULDN'T you want a Square Foot Garden instead of a traditional (which is to say, inefficient, wasteful and time-consuming) row garden? You see, compared to single row gardening, you get 100 percent of the harvest with only:

40 percent of the cost

20 percent of the space

10 percent of the water

5 percent of the seeds

2 percent of the work

No Weeds

Pretty strong argument for an SFG, right? But that's not all. When you plant an SFG, there's no fretting about your soil because we recommend you use Mel's Mix, a special blend that's easy to create and that you can use without fuss. No rototilling, no testing, no fertilizing. SFGs can also be started in any season and can be built to accommodate just about any physical limitation. In fact, we've pretty much removed the hard work from gardening and left the enjoyment! They are great ways to share a positive experience with all family members and promote a healthy, enjoyable lifestyle.

2. How is the ALL NEW Square Foot Gardening method better than the original?

I've made 10 major improvements to the method, to help make SFG even more foolproof than ever.

1. New Location: Close to the House
2. New Direction: Up, Not Down
3. New Soil: Mel's Mix
4. New Depth: Only 6 inches Deep
5. No Fertilizer: You Don't Need It
6. New Boxes: Above the Ground
7. New Aisles: Comfortable Width
8. New Grids: Prominent and Permanent
9. New Idea: Don't Waste Seeds
10. New Opportunities: Tabletop Gardens

With the ALL NEW SFG, you reduce the size of your garden and tuck it up next to the house so that you're more likely to enjoy and maintain it. I've eliminated all the digging you would have otherwise had to do, along with the tools you would need. Instead, you'll need just 6 inches of Mel's Mix soil, boxes made from reclaimed or common lumber, and a permanent grid to affix to the top of your box. You can even put a bottom on your box and move it to a new location—even to the top of a table!

? 3. How do I get started?

! Just like shopping for real estate, successful SFG begins with the right location. Find a spot away from trees and shrubs. It should receive six to eight hours of direct sun per day. It should also drain well, so that water doesn't puddle after a heavy rain. Then build a basic box and fill it with Mel's Mix, made of equal parts of blended compost, coarse vermiculite and peat moss. Finish your SFG by adding a grid on top of your box, because if it doesn't have a grid, it's not a Square Foot Garden. A grid is so important to the many parts of Square Foot Gardening, it's not just decorative. Without it you won't fully practice all the advantages of this innovative system.

? 4. How much of each crop can I plant in the squares?

! Planting your SFG is all about growing a diversity of your favorite fruits, vegetables, and flowers, and giving your crops exactly the space they need. You'll poke holes and plant seeds in each square depending on the mature plant's size: 1, 4, 9, or 16 holes per square. Smaller plants such as radishes and carrots—or any with a recommended spacing of 3 inches or less—will be planted a pinch (two or three seeds) to a square. Medium-size plants, including spinach, turnips, and bush beans to name a few, will require nine plants per square.

Large plants requiring 6-inch spacing, such as leaf lettuce and parsley, will be planted four to a square. Finally, extra large plants such as broccoli, cauliflower, cabbages, tomatoes, and bell peppers will be given an entire square of their very own.

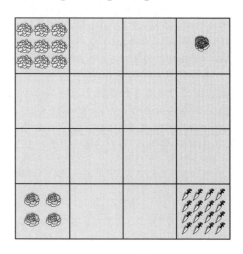

Lay out your SFG box with a variety of plants, planting the number per square based on the "thinned spacing" listed on the seed packet.

5. I have a lot of seeds left. Can I save them for next year?

You bet. One of the great things about SFG is that it conserves resources—along with your money. Because SFG uses only a pinch of seeds—basically just those that will become mature plants—you should store the extra seeds for use in the future. Just be careful to store them correctly: keep seeds in a cool, dry place. I always recommend refrigerating them in wide-mouth glass jars with screw lids. (Mason jars or resealable plastic bags are perfect!) Add a dessicant (drying agent) to each jar, such as the small silica packets from aspirin bottles, or uncooked rice, or a small amount of powdered milk wrapped up in tissue paper. Then label the jars or bags and group them by type before you put them in an out-of-the way area of your refrigerator for storage.

6. Is 6 inches of soil really enough to grow in? What about potatoes and carrots?

You should see the eyebrows shoot up when I tell audiences they only need 6 inches of soil for the vast majority of crops they'll grow. But it's true. However, a few root crops, such as potatoes and carrots, require deeper soil. To give them what they need, we go up instead of down in SFG, saving the gardener a lot of digging. I call the solution a Top Hat Box. The box helps Square Foot Gardeners grow beautiful long carrots with ease. It measures 1 foot × 1 foot × 6 inches deep, and is placed on top of a single square of your regular SFG box, effectively doubling the depth of that square foot. Fill the Top Hat Box with Mel's Mix and grow carrots to your heart's delight! To grow perfect potatoes, place 4 inches of Mel's mix in a square, with 2 inches of pure compost on top. Plant the potatoes in the compost layer, four to a square. Once the plants have grown 1 inch above the surface, place the Top Hat Box over the square and add 2 inches of Mel's Mix. Keep adding 2 inches of soil every time the potato plants grow 1 inch, until the box is full.

⑦ 7. What is Mel's Mix?

Mel's Mix is the magical soil formula at the heart of SFG's success. It is a perfectly balanced blend of three ingredients that provides all the nutrients your crops will need, with ideal moisture-retention properties. It also saves you a whole lot of effort and time you might have spent digging and improving your existing soil.

The Mel's Mix formula is about as simple as they come:
1 part blended compost
1 part peat moss
1 part coarse vermiculite
Simply mix up the equal parts (by volume, not weight) and your soil is ready!

⑧ 8. Does it have to be compost? What if I don't have the space or ability to make compost? Does it really have to be five different types?

You can't get better soil than general compost. It has all the nutrients your plants need to grow, and a loose and friable structure that makes it easy to work and quick-draining. I like homemade compost because all the different ingredients ensure a full range of nutrients. It's pretty darn easy to make a compost pile . . . and it's free! However, if you can't compost for some reason, you should buy at least five different types of compost and mix them together. That will ensure that your plants get a blended mix of all the nutrients and minerals they need. When the plants are happy, the gardener's happy!

❓ 9. Where do I find coarse vermiculite?

❗ Depending on where you live, you may have to search a bit to find this crucial Mel's Mix ingredient. Many larger home improvement centers carry 4-cubic-foot bags. If your local center doesn't, I'd suggest you look under "Greenhouse Supplies" in the Yellow Pages, or online. I'd also warn you that there will be labels on the vermiculite and peat moss that are both very dusty. That's why I always tell gardeners to wear a painter's dust mask, gloves and eye protection when blending your Mel's Mix, and only mix it outdoors on a calm day with little or no wind.

❓ 10. How can I become a certified instructor of Square Foot Gardening?

❗ One of our favorite functions of the Square Foot Gardening Foundation is helping people become SFG instructors who spread the word. The best way to learn how to teach the method is through one of our three-day symposiums held throughout the year in different cities across the country. Of course, if you can't make a symposium, we understand. In that case, you can take our new online course, or follow a home study course through our correspondence program. See our website, www. squarefootgardening.org for more details.

THE SFG TIMELINE

1975   Mel Bartholomew organizes a community garden as a retirement project.

1976   As a result of his experiences, Mel develops and introduces the Square Foot Gardening Method.

1981   Due to the increasing popularity of SFG, Mel writes about his method, and the original *Square Foot Gardening* is published.

1982   Mel promotes the book and is seen and approached by PBS to film several one-minute video spots in Mel's garden. The spots prove so popular, Mel begins filming a 30-minute, weekly national show.

1989   One year after bringing his PBS show to a close and retiring for the second time, Mel is approached by Discovery Channel to launch a new show. Second retirement ends even quicker than the first.

1991   Mel retires for the third time!

| 1996 | Mel establishes a foundation to help teachers teach SFG to schoolchildren: the program is called "A Square Yard in the School Yard". |

| 1998 | Mel commits the SFG Foundation to putting an SFG in every grammar school in Utah. It takes 3 years, but they succeed! |

| 2001 | The SFG Foundation creates "Square Meter Gardening" to help Third World countries improve nutrition, prevent starvation and increase independence. |

| 2005 | Mel finishes writing *All New Square Foot Gardening.* It goes on to be his second bestseller. |

| 2009 | Mel writes the *All New Square Foot Gardening Cookbook.* |

| The present... | The SFG ideal has spread throughout America and across the globe. Mel and the SFG foundation train SFG teachers, work to expand Square Yard in the School Yard programs, and grow the global Square Meter Gardening movement. |

| ...and beyond! | With the publication of the *All New Square Foot Gardening Answer Book*, Mel continues his mission to help people around the world conserve resources, grow more in less space, work less and enjoy more, and understand all aspects of Square Foot Gardening! |

PLANNING & LOCATING YOUR SQUARE FOOT GARDEN

Real estate agents like to say that the three most important things affecting a home's value are "location, location, and location." Same is true of an SFG. If you were growing an old-fashioned row garden, chances are you'd just stick it out at the far edge of your backyard and not worry if part of it was too shaded to grow. Long rows usually only fit in one part of your yard, which means the type of gardening you do is dictated by the location.

Not so with an SFG. Because your SFG boxes take up so much less square footage than a row garden (and produce just as much in that area, I might add!), the issue of location is pretty wide open. You do, however, need to make sure the entire box will get at least six to eight hours of sunlight each day, and that it's properly shaded from strong winds and harsh weather.

Locating SFG boxes was actually one of the big changes I made to the method when I was working on the *ALL NEW Square Foot Gardening* book. It had become crystal clear to me that the closer SFG boxes were to the gardener's back door, or right below the kitchen window, the more likely the gardener was to work on them and enjoy them.

As soon as that book came out, though, you can bet that a bunch of questions followed. Most started with, "Yeah, but what if. . . ." Every yard is unique and everybody's situation is going to be different. Some people might have a deck or patio out their back door, and they just don't want to put an SFG box on the surface (although I sure wish they would—an SFG is a wonderful addition to any deck or patio).

Finding just the right location makes for a lot of questions, and I've included them all in this chapter. When you're planning what you'll plant and where, however, you'll need to consider the location of the boxes, as well as the individual squares

> *"When I sold my house, the buyer said, 'I bought your house for your garden.' SFG of course."*
>
> —Michelle from El Cesjon

inside the boxes. Position taller plants in squares where they won't shade out lower-growing types. Also, separating the plants of the same type will help alleviate pests and diseases.

Creating the perfect mix of plants and positioning them in just the right squares of your box takes a bit of thinking. A lot of questions are bound to come up and I'll answer the most common ones here. Once you've arrived at the answers, you're sure to find the perfect place for your boxes, and the perfect place within your boxes for your plants.

❓ I live in Arizona. How can I keep my SFG healthy in the desert?

❗ One of the great things about SFGs is that they work just about anywhere! You'd be surprised at all the places where I've seen them. You can grow a healthy SFG even in a desert climate with just a few simple steps. Once your plants are growing and established, the first order of business is to lay down a thick layer of water-conserving mulch. This can be wet newspapers or cardboard, chopped-up straw, or even dried grass clippings. Some people use black plastic, but you might want to cover it with another mulch material—there's no reason your SFG should be anything but beautiful. Conventional mulch, such as wood chips or bark, will work as well. However, whenever I use wood chips in an SFG, I always put down a barrier first because wood chips can pull nitrogen from the soil as they decompose and your plants aren't going to be real happy about that.

In a desert environment, wind can be as much a concern as the sun. We've had a lot of success making wind screens from the floating cover type of cloth material sold at nurseries and large garden centers. Stick a steel fence post outside each corner of the 4 × 4 square and then wrap the cloth around the stakes and the box sides, just like you see them do around a tennis court.

You should always keep in mind to treat your plants like people and make them as comfortable as possible wherever your SFG happens to be. In that case you might even put up some sort of shade for the extreme noontime sun. I'm sure the plants would appreciate that, as well as a little extra water as necessary. You can also look into a drip irrigation system.

Can I grow a Square Foot Garden in my very shady yard?

There's just no getting around the fact that every yard is different. If you have a two-story house, it may block the sun for a good portion of the day (part of my new SFG method is to move your boxes close to the house). Sometimes trees can be the problem—and most people just aren't ready to cut down their trees to suit their garden. I understand that. But to grow vegetables and most flowers successfully, you're going to need the equivalent of six to eight hours of sun on your plants every single day. I say "the equivalent" because there are tricks you can use to help your plants make the most of what sun there is.

If you don't mind the appearance, one of the best ways to optimize your sunlight is to line the ground around your plants with white Styrofoam panels. Not only will the panels bounce a lot of sunlight back up on your plants, they will also serve as a moisture-evaporating barrier and can even work to repel insects! (The light bouncing up under the plant leaves confuses insects that expect that area to be darker and concealing.)

If you're willing to go a bit further with the idea, and your garden is against the fence or house, you can even line a fence along the northeast or west side of the garden with Styrofoam panels. Or better yet, tie them to the fence. That way, you can take them down whenever you're having company or just don't feel like looking at a bright white surface. It may sound like a bit much, but it's one way to make the most of a shady location. If Styrofoam isn't to your taste, you can always limit your plants to those that do better in shade, such as beets, carrots, cauliflower, Swiss chard, lettuce, onions, parsley, radishes, spinach, hosta, coleus, and many herbs (just check your seed catalog or packages). Although it's not the ideal garden, these can all make do with as little as four to six hours of sun a day.

⑦ My yard is flat and bare and no matter where I place my SFG it receives bright, strong sun throughout the day. How can I protect my plants?

❗ Too much of a good thing can be a bad thing, especially when it comes to bright, hot sunshine and your summer plants. Providing just a little bit of protection from the sun during the hottest part of the day is probably all you need to do to make sure your SFG doesn't come down with a bad case of heat stroke. The easiest way to cast a welcome bit of shade over the plants is by building a sun screen. Get your hands on some ½-inch PVC pipes 10 feet long. Bend them to opposite corners to form two parallel hoops over your SFG box, then tie them together right at the top center points. Then all you need to do is attach a bit of shade cloth that you can find at home centers or garden supply outlets. That will allow you to adjust the cloth as necessary to give your plants some much-needed midday relief when the sun is at its most scorching.

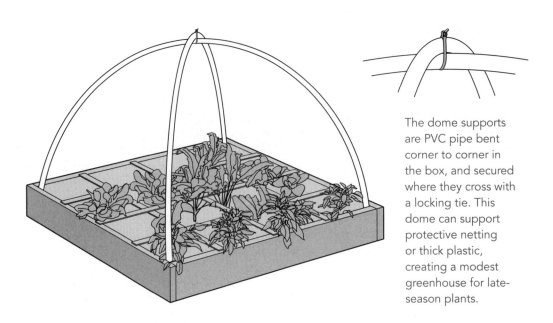

The dome supports are PVC pipe bent corner to corner in the box, and secured where they cross with a locking tie. This dome can support protective netting or thick plastic, creating a modest greenhouse for late-season plants.

Can I grow my SFG indoors?

Certainly you can. A sunroom or even a sunny area in a big eat-in kitchen is an ideal place for a little winter garden. An SFG can also be a great indoor project in a school or hospital. In any case, though, you should build the boxes so that they can pass through doorways: 3-foot-wide maximum for commercial buildings like a hospital, and 2-foot-wide maximum for homes. The plants will bend toward the sun, so you should rotate the box every week or so. With the reduced light of winter, don't expect plush, bushy plants. But the effort is still worthwhile in a cold drab winter. Pick plants and varieties that do well in shade or reduced light (check your seed catalogs).

MEL'S TIP

It makes me happy to see how many people have embraced SFG, and I love the fact that they get together online in chat rooms and forums to discuss their experiences. But there's a reason we certify SFG instructors; it's a simple method but you still have to know your stuff! It's fine to check out what works for others, but if you have a particular problem or concern, I say go right to an expert. You can consult your local Cooperative Extension Service agent or a local nursery professional for local plant and pest problems, or go to the SFG forum for SFG problems. Always be aware of the difference between what someone knows, and what someone thinks.

Where is the most unusual location you've ever seen a Square Foot Garden grown?

I'd have to say it was in the Himalayan Mountains in India. It was amazing to be that far from home and see something so familiar. It also made me realize that SFG transcends language and cultural barriers. Every person around the world needs fresh food to eat and

Continued

can benefit by growing their own food. Our foundation's mission is to encourage EVERY household to have just one Square Metre box for each person right out their back door. Let us, for the first time in history, teach the world how to grow just the minimum of food themselves and we will have taken a big step toward eliminating world hunger by increasing independence.

What's the best way to place my SFG on a slope?

When it comes to your yard's geography, there are slopes, and then there are SLOPES. If the slope you're talking about is a couple inches or so for every 10 feet of yard, you'll be fine just setting your SFG boxes in place a little bit out of level. However, if your yard slopes more than 6 inches per 10 feet, you're going have to take some corrective measures with your SFG boxes.

Really, it comes down to whether you want to change the yard, or your boxes. Where the slope is severe enough that you'll need to level the boxes, but not steep like the side of a hill, I'd suggest kind of "terracing" your yard—digging out a flat area underneath each box so that it sits level. That won't work so well if you have a severe slope, because dirt and yard debris on the uphill side will always be tumbling into your box. Water runoff will also be a problem. If the water flows downhill fast enough, it can even wash out some of your Mel's Mix, which is the last thing we want! In this case, I'd suggest adding a solid plywood bottom to each box, and two legs on the downhill side so that the box sits level, but the uphill edge of the box sits above ground level.

You can also place the boxes along a path at the top or bottom of the slope. Just keep in mind you may be limited in how far you can reach in from the "up-slope" side; you may want to make your boxes 2 or 3 feet wide to account for this limited access. One last word on sloped yards; a lot of times they are wasted, unusable space. By cutting in a wide terrace 8 to 10 feet deep, you might create both a great place for your SFG boxes and a more usable patio area.

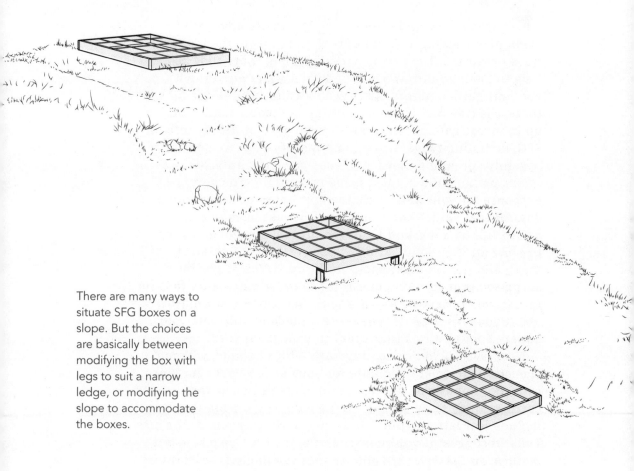

There are many ways to situate SFG boxes on a slope. But the choices are basically between modifying the box with legs to suit a narrow ledge, or modifying the slope to accommodate the boxes.

My yard has lots of old-growth trees—can I still plan my SFG around them?

As you may know, one thing I strongly advocate when placing your SFG boxes is NOT to locate them near trees or shrubs. The fact is, trees have big roots that just long to push up into the delicious Mel's Mix and crowd out your garden plants. Also, with all that new water up there, the tree will sense something is up and send roots up to investigate. Trees can also drop a lot of debris into an SFG, including twigs, leaves, and insects—not to mention possibly spreading disease to your garden plants.

But perhaps the biggest issue is sunlight. The very best exposure for your SFG is six to eight hours of direct sun a day. All that said, I know some people just have to deal with a yard full of trees, and I'd never suggest someone not try to grow an SFG. So let's think about ways to do it. First, try to find the sunniest spots in the yard. You might be surprised that the sun penetrates to certain areas—wherever that is, you're talking about a good SFG box location. How about your front yard? What better place to show off your Square Foot abilities than right in your front yard.

Next, even if you're dealing with a bit of shade, you can choose shade-tolerant plants for your SFG. Say, for instance, coleus or impatiens, and root crops like radishes and carrots. Many leafy greens can also do okay in shade; these include leaf lettuces and Swiss chard. Here is something else I would suggest if you're forced to place your boxes near a mature tree: attach plywood bottoms on the boxes. That way the trees pesky roots aren't going to be a problem, and you can easily move the box to test out different exposures in different areas. Heck, you can even put out a couple of chairs and make a little patio setting! If things don't grow at all, well, you'll know that the shade is just too dense.

❓ Do I need to place my boxes as close to each other as possible?

❗ One of the terrific things about an SFG is the fact that because it's so much smaller than a row garden, you have a lot more options as far as where it can go—including separating different SFG boxes in the same yard. You can put one here, one there, one on the porch, one alongside the garage—just about anywhere that the box gets the right amount of sun. Some folks do find it easier to have the boxes together—so that they can see what's going at any one time with a glance, and so that they can do all the tending of the garden without moving around too much.

If you're going to have several boxes together, make sure you have plenty of working room. But I say, plan and position your boxes where your crops will grow best and in the places that make you happiest. You might want the flowers to brighten up an empty corner of your backyard, so you plant one SFG with all flowering plants and put it in that corner. Maybe you want herbs and vegetables close by so you can pick them as you're making dinner. Put them right by the back door leading onto a deck. That's just another way of taking advantage of all SFG has to offer!

❓ What's the best way to plan for growing winter crops?

❗ Make life easy on yourself by picking one specific SFG box and saying, "This will be my cold-weather box." When fall rolls around, plant it entirely with the cold-weather leaf and root crops. This is one of the great things about the condensed size of a SFG: it's easier to protect cold-weather crops in a single box. Provide adequate protection—like the hoop frame described on page 22, covered with thick plastic sheeting and a blanket. Now you'll have salad fixings right through Thanksgiving, and maybe even Christmas!

What is the best way to plan out the crops for my SFG?

I think the easiest way for most gardeners to plan out their crops is to just draw a big square with a grid of 16 squares inside, to represent each SFG box. Then all you do is label the squares with what you want to grow in them. To start out, work in pencil because you may need to adjust your plans. This gives you the chance to play with different combinations of plantings and ensure what we call "selective separation"—growing the same crops in different boxes so that anything affecting one square won't easily spread and affect another crop nearby. It's also wise to label the squares with the number of plants per square foot, so you can get a sense of how full the overall SFG box will be. You can also graph out different versions of the same box, to show the transition plantings as you move through the seasons. (Some people even color code the squares!) Keep an eye out for the basics, such as putting taller plants on the north side of the box. Put plants that require a lot of attention, grooming, or harvesting (like bush beans) near the outside, and low-maintenance plants like radishes and carrots (plant and pull) on the inside squares.

Once you lay out your SFG box with crops, it's easy to see just how much bounty one box can provide.

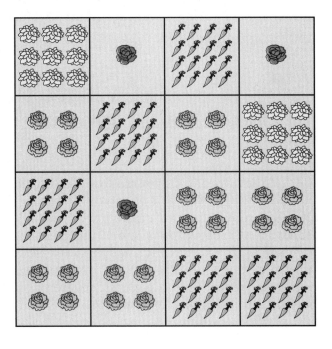

28

How should I site my SFG to work around my swimming pool?

Look for a flat area close to the water, but not in the way of traffic. If people have to walk around the box or boxes, chances are that they will eventually walk right through them. But I think boxes are a great addition to any kind of water feature. Set them by a pool for an interesting look and a quick snack for hungry swimmers! Position them on either side of a manmade stream, and you have a handy water source for watering the boxes whenever they need it. One last suggestion I have for you, though, is to consider incorporating the water feature right into the SFG box itself!

I designed a pyramid of SFG boxes for the Salt Lake City Flower and Garden Show one year. It had a 1 × 1 box on top of a 2 × 2 box, on top of a 3 × 3 box, all of which sat on a base of a 4 × 4 box. The top box was a little pool, with a liner holding the water, and even a few fish swimming around in the box. We ran a tube that siphoned the water down over the side and through the different squares, with a pump at the bottom that pumped the water back up to the top square. It was the hit of the entire show, and people continually crowded around and just kept watching the whole display like they thought something spectacular was going to happen any minute. Photographers had to ask people to step back so that they could get a picture for their newspaper or magazine. It was all done with hidden plastic tubes, and you could easily create your own water feature pyramid like that at home, with supplies from the local home center.

What's the most creative SFG box layout you've ever seen?

A couple of the most creative were boxes I built for people in the suburbs of Salt Lake City, Utah. People would often come by and say, "I want to convert my whole backyard to SFG." Much as I admired their sentiment, I had to warn them against growing too much. (Remember "100 percent of the harvest in 20 percent of the space"?) Just the same, I had some fun with those designs. For one yard, I put 2-foot-wide boxes all around the perimeter fence. Every 6 to 8 feet, we'd come out with a 4 × 4 or 4 × 6 "pier" that still left plenty of room to reach in and tend the garden.

Then in each corner, I would step up the 2-foot-wide perimeter box so the corner was 2 or 3 feet higher, and step down as it continued along the fence. The owner was ecstatic over the look. Another lady wanted a design centered on a big pathway down the center of her backyard. So what we did was put an arbor right down the center, leaving the path 6 feet wide so that two people could walk along side by side. We ran 4 × 16 boxes out from each side, stepped down. So, at the arbor, they were 3 feet high for easy harvest, and then every 4 feet along, they'd be stepped down a foot. We put nylon netting to grow vertical crops over the arbor. It turned out quite nicely. You can find pictures of other interesting SFG designs on our website at www.squarefootgardening.org.

In the end though, you can make just about any design that you can imagine. However, I would strongly suggest you limit the actual number of boxes to those you can reasonably care for and use the harvest from. Too much can be almost as bad as too little in the garden.

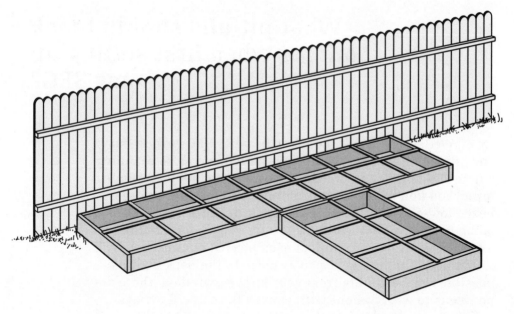

A "pier" design as shown here is just one of many different ways to configure your SFG boxes. Whatever design you choose, though, make sure you don't build more boxes than you can tend.

MEL'S TIP

Sometimes your first Square Foot Garden can be so exciting and you're so enthused that you overbuild it. Remember I've seen people that turn their whole backyards into Square Foot boxes—all kinds of fancy things. It was gorgeous, beautiful! But they couldn't take care of it, and they couldn't get rid of everything, so they gradually converted all the vegetables into flowers, which didn't take as much care, but was still too much garden for the space.

Here's what I suggest. Whether you're a beginner or an expert, lay out a plan and break it up into phase one and phase two. That way you'll have an easy start to it and won't be overwhelmed the first year. Then the second year you can add on to it according to your master plan.

🔵 What pitfalls should I look out for when first setting up my SFG?

🔴 Well, there aren't too many because SFGs are so easy and simple to set up. I would say that when you're planning where you're going to put the boxes, **always keep traffic in mind**. You don't want people or pets walking through the boxes to get to another part of the yard, and if your SFG is going to be in a busy yard, make sure you plan on building a chicken-wire cage to protect each box. Of course, we recommend that the boxes go as close to the back door as possible and be visible from your kitchen window (there are no weeds to worry about with your SFG, so you'll always want to show it off!), but that will depend on what direction the house faces and how much sun that particular area gets.

The one other mistake common to new Square Foot Gardeners is making their gardens too big. **Start small.** Learn the system. Chances are you don't need (and probably can't use) as much as you think you need. First time Square Foot Gardeners are always amazed at how much they can grow in such a small space, so don't convert the whole backyard in one fell swoop! Start with one or two boxes, and if the season goes well, you can always increase your harvest for next season.

Do I need to do anything differently in order to to put my box on my deck?

Now there's something you can't do with a row garden! There's really nothing special you need do except that any time you position an SFG box on a solid surface like a deck or patio, you need to put a bottom on it. Plain old plywood will work best; use ⅜-inch plywood for smaller boxes such as 3 × 3s, and sturdier ½-inch or ¾-inch plywood for bigger boxes like 4 × 4s. Make sure you drill the right number of drainage holes—one per square foot and one in each corner. Of course, those **drainage holes** need to be able to drain, right? On some flat surfaces, like a cement slab or tiled patio, the holes might be blocked. In that case, you should put a small spacer under the box.

What's a spacer? Just about anything you have on hand. A couple of pebbles put under one side of the box will work just fine. The pebbles will raise the box up enough so that the water can drain freely out of the drainage holes. The other thing I tell people to look out for when they're putting SFG boxes on patios or porches is **traffic**. Decks and patios are usually pretty popular places and see a lot of foot traffic. Make sure your box is well out of the way so it doesn't get accidentally stepped on or otherwise abused.

I really like the idea of placing a box right by the back door on a patio or deck. That way, when you're cooking and you say, "Oh, I need some herbs," you can just step outside and snip off some fresh basil, lemon verbena, or parsley! Or pull a few bright red-and-white radishes to surprise guests. You could even ask them to pull a few for dinner while you finish setting the table. Picture that!

Do SFG boxes have to be square?

I absolutely love fun shapes and I'm all for being creative with your SFG, just as long as you have the room and you leave the right amount of space around the boxes so that you can reach into them. Diamonds, for example, take a lot more space and don't leave room for an organized path, but if your yard is spacious, diamond configurations (squares that are turned) can look very nice.

There are actually all kinds of different layouts you can use to spice up the look of your SFG and your yard in general. You don't even have to always think in squares. For instance, you might have a nice 4-foot-wide aisle down the center of your yard, with 4 × 8 or 4 × 12 (a great size for a family) boxes perpendicular to the aisle.

You can also put boxes at angles for all kinds of different looks. And as long as we're talking about creative layouts, why not think in three dimensions? One of the most interesting boxes I ever put together was at our Thanksgiving Point Display Garden in Salt Lake City. We made a 4 × 16 box with step-ups every 4 feet. So the first 4 feet of the box was 6 inches deep, the next 4-foot section was 12 inches deep and so on. You can do a lot with stepped boxes—maybe step up every 2 feet, or every foot! One thing for sure your plants aren't going to worry about—they won't get dizzy if they're raised up, and they won't get confused if they're in a diamond box.

I'd love to start an SFG but I live in an apartment. Can I plant my SFG on the roof?

As long as it's safe, a roof can be an ideal place for an SFG because roofs get a lot of sun. The roof has to be able to support the weight of the box, but usually, if it can support an average adult walking on it, it will have no problem supporting the weight of an SFG box. You'll need a safe way to get up on the roof regularly, and you'll need to run some sort of hose or water source up to the roof, because I don't think you're going to want to be lugging pails of water up four flights of stairs!

The top of the building isn't the only roof you can use though. We had one young couple who planted a beautiful SFG on the roof of the carport over the cars in their apartment complex. They just put up a ladder in their parking area and went up every day after work to garden. I would recommend that you put any rooftop SFG boxes on legs—they can be bricks or cinder blocks for all it matters— to ensure the boxes can drain properly, and so you don't get blamed for any leaks in the roof.

You should also keep boxes far away from the roof edge for safety's sake. And in every case, make sure you have written permission from the building manager to use the roof for a garden. Your SFG won't be of much use to you if you wind up getting kicked out of your apartment!

How can I plan my SFG to make it fun for the whole family?

I like the way you're thinking, not only because many hands make for quick work, but also because the SFG method is so incredibly adaptable to everyone's needs. For the kids or grandkids in your house, plan on building one or two 3 × 3 "square yard" boxes (the smaller size makes it easier for the kids to reach into the box). When you begin choosing the plants for the squares, I'd include the little ones in that planning. Children always have great ideas about what they want in their boxes, and the process of choosing plants is a great way to explain how different plants grow, all about seasons, and the basic biology of gardening.

You can also plan a box or two for older or physically challenged members of the house. A tabletop box can be just the ticket for a grandma or grandpa who might need a scooter or wheelchair to get around. If your husband's bad hip (from playing all that golf) makes it tough for him to get down and garden in your regular SFG boxes, build a higher "standing" box, from 34 to 36 inches above the ground.

Is there a way I can pest-proof my SFG boxes when I start them?

You've asked the right question at the right time. All too often, the folks at the SFG Foundation receive panicked phone calls or emails along the lines of, "Help! The raccoons are stealing my strawberries." After your fruit or vegetables start disappearing, or your plants are already damaged, is simply the wrong time to start taking action.

Of course, the action you take should depend on the pests and problems you're most likely to encounter in your little corner of the world. Rural locations are more likely to deal with wildlife, while each individual region of the country has its own particular pests to deal with. In any case, your first line of defense is location. Place your box right outside your kitchen window where you see it perhaps several times a day, and you're more likely to detect problems as soon as they arise and nip them in the bud, so to speak. If you're worried about pets, larger problems such as deer, or your yard just happens to be the gathering place for your children's friends, you might want to start right out with a chicken wire cover for your SFG box (see page 51).

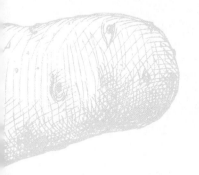

I'd like to plan out my water usage. Could you tell me how many gallons an SFG will consume per day, per square foot?

Only if you tell me how long a piece of string is. You see, it's an open-ended question because you'd need to know what piece of string I was talking about. In the same way, I'd need to know what plants you'll be planting, your local climate, and many other factors. Even then, I don't think it is a very helpful exercise. The most important thing to keep in mind is that an SFG saves almost 90 percent of the water you would use in a row garden.

Your water needs will change over time as a plant matures. An adult plant needs a lot more water than a seedling. And different plants have different requirements. A melon plant generally requires more water than a square filled with carrots. See how many variables there are? You can rest easily, however, knowing that because of the specific makeup of Mel's Mix, every drop of water that goes into your SFG is being efficiently used—held until it can be sipped up by plant roots, with extra water being allowed to drain down. Careful watering is your best conservation method—if you poke your finger into the soil, it should feel moist. If it's dry, add a little water. It's why I recommend always keeping a pail of sun-warmed water right next to each SFG bed.

Can I plan to put my SFG right on top of my grass?

You certainly can. Here's what you do: mow the grass as low as possible, **lay your weed fabric right over top of the grass,** then set your box in place. That's the easy way. If you're willing to do a bit more work, I'd suggest you remove the grass under where your SFG boxes will be placed. This will head off any problems with tenacious grass growing up through the bottom of your box. (Cheap weed cloth lets any vigorous weed through after a year or two. So spend a little money and get professional-grade fabric.) In either case, you can leave the grass outside the box alone, as a soft surface for the aisles between your boxes. Just mow it like it is part of your lawn, which it is. If your mower can't get right up beside the box, a weed trimmer works wonders and is very quick and easy to use.

Can I have an SFG on my tiny apartment balcony?

Certainly. It's all a matter of adapting the method to your circumstances. First of all, the balcony has to receive six to eight hours of sun daily. If you have permission from the landlord, you can bolt 6-inch-wide SFG boxes to a wood railing, or use special hangers—available from nurseries and garden centers—to **hang boxes** on the inside of just about any railing. Obviously, the squares are not going to be "square foot" but the principles are all the same. If you have room on the floor of the balcony, you can place your modified SFG boxes right on the floor—and even grow tomatoes on netting attached to the box and the inside of the railing!

❓ I'd like to make my SFG boxes a little deeper than 6 inches, with more soil. Is that a problem?

❗ I don't suppose "problem" is the right word. "Unnecessary" is the word I would use. You can certainly make your boxes as deep as you want and add as much soil as you like, but you always have to ask yourself, "Do I really need that?" **More isn't always better.** Quite honestly, if it were quantifiably better to have deeper boxes with more soil, I would have designed the system for just that. Instead, I designed SFG to be as efficient and cost-effective as possible. You really only need to use 1 × 6 or 2 × 6 lumber and fill up the box with 6 inches (well, 5½ inches because of the nominal lumber size) of high quality Mel's Mix soil. Fill it to the top and I guarantee you, you will have all the soil you need to grow practically any crops you want. We even have a good solution for growing 12-inch carrots in 6 inches of soil.

❓ My entire yard is paved—can I still grow some sort of SFG?

❗ You can grow a full-fledged SFG. Just think of your yard as one big patio—and **there are plenty of patio SFGs.** You need to build your boxes with plywood bottoms on them, and drill drainage holes in the plywood (one in every square foot and one at each corner). Then place them where they are the closest to your house, get the most sun, and are still protected from wind and adverse weather. Remember if we don't use our existing soil, there's no reason to dig it. It doesn't matter what kind of surface it is is—rocks, gravel, cement, wood deck. No matter what, Square Foot Gardening still works.

❓ I'd love to grow an SFG, but I'm not sure I can afford to. How much do they cost?

❗ What's to afford? If you absolutely can't spend any money whatsoever, you can still Square Foot Garden. First, you'll need lumber for the boxes, and larger cutoff pieces can work for this. You can find that at a construction site (ask the site supervisor or foreman before taking any wood). You'll probably find lots of possible sides for your boxes, even cut to exactly the 4-foot length you need.

Next, if money is a problem, you can grow your crops in pure compost, and you can make your own compost. No need to get fancy in building a compost bin—find old, broken pallets behind a supermarket or large retailer and stand them up in a box shape, then tie the four corners together with scrap twine both top and bottom to make your FREE compost bin. Although it's not ideal, neither are we! Fill the boxes with the FREE compost you have collected from all the stuff people throw out and pretty soon you're ready to Square Foot Garden!

You don't even need to buy tools—I'm betting you have an inexpensive pair of scissors (children's scissors are the best), a pencil, and an old trowel. Just to show you how adaptable Square Foot Gardening is, in a Third World country we don't even have trowels—we use sticks. How? Because Mel's Mix, or even just compost, stays loose and friable. A few packets of seeds will cost you less than a latte, and you'll be good to go. You don't need fertilizer, and you're going to use very little water, so it shouldn't affect your utilities bill. And when the crop comes in, expect to save money on groceries!

Even though I've worked it out on graph paper, I'm still not sure I've picked the best spot for my SFG boxes. How can I be sure?

First things first. I don't want you to lose any sleep about where your boxes wind up, because ultimately, they're portable no matter what. But if you're having a hard time envisioning how the boxes would look in your yard, there's another way you can "see" the layout. Go down to a bicycle shop or appliance store. They've got all kinds of big boxes they throw out. Bring a couple of those home, cut out a piece of 4 × 4-foot cardboard, and lay that down with a brick on top to hold it down. Now, spending no money and doing no damage to the lawn you can see very well all the boxes. Look at those boxes from the top floor of your house, from the neighbor's yard, and from other perspectives. This also gives you a chance to see what kind of sun exposure your boxes will receive.

Once you're happy with the location, ask for comments from the peanut gallery—your spouse, kids, neighbors, and friends. You might be surprised at what they have to say. One of your children or grandchildren might point out, "You know, we can't play soccer in the yard anymore." Or someone else will say, "The dog is going to run right over that." A fresh pair of eyes can often see challenges or issues you might never have thought about. If you decide to change locations, it's as simple as moving the cardboard. Once you're entirely happy with the locations, you're ready to go ahead and place your boxes.

Now if you or someone in your household is real finicky, here's another idea. After you did all of the above and you are sure of the box sizes you have selected, go ahead and put your boxes together and place them over the locations you have laid out. If you bought your boxes from our website, all you have to do is push the sides together and drop in a pin (our boxes require no tools to assemble). Next add the grids on the tops of all the boxes and NOW, stand back and after observing for a day or two, well, look around and thank all your family and neighbors who said it wouldn't work. Of course, someone will suggest that if you move just that one box over 2½ feet, it will be perfect.

CHAPTER 2

BUILDING YOUR SFG BOXES

A big part of writing the *ALL NEW Square Foot Gardening* book was outlining some mighty important changes to the way SFG boxes were built and used. The idea of portable boxes that can be positioned in a lot of different ways is key to the improvements I've made to the SFG method. Of course, that means I get asked a lot of questions about boxes when I travel around the country meeting different Square Foot Gardeners (and potential Square Foot Gardeners, which is just about everybody).

The questions usually start with the materials that can be used to build the boxes. I call this "inside the box" thinking, and I really enjoy seeing people get creative with what they use—or reuse!—to build their boxes. More often than not, though, the questions are about what types of materials are acceptable and which aren't. That's an important distinction and I'm happy to talk about the do's and don'ts of building SFG boxes.

Beyond the materials, actual box construction is a hotter topic than ever before. Because I modified the method so that gardeners no longer have to dig down into the existing soil, their SFG boxes can be moved to just about anywhere the gardener wants them to go. That opens up a whole world of possibilities, but it also leads to a world of questions. Ultimately, it's about making

"We are in our first season of growing Square Foot Gardens and are hooked on it. We have nine kids and . . . 10 garden boxes: five are 4 × 8 and five are 4 × 12. The veggies and flowers have grown prodigiously in an extremely short time, and we are eating yummy things every day. Our daughters keep our house full of bouquets from our Square Foot Garden. Everyone who sees our gardens is quite impressed. Thank you!"

—Brenda in Michigan

portability as easy and simple as possible, while still ensuring those precious plants get all the sun and care that they need. There are many ways to do that, and we're developing more all the time.

Most box questions these days, though, are all about situating boxes for special conditions or in special places. Because Square Foot Gardeners can now put a bottom on a box, the boxes can be used to accommodate seated or standing gardeners. Boxes can be stacked, put on tables, built with legs, or even terraced. There are just all kinds of possibilities. We're even thinking of treehouses, but then of course, there's the sun problem.

The questions in this chapter cover the range of what our teachers and professionals get asked again and again about SFG boxes. I think if you read through it rather than cherry pick individual questions and answers, you'll get a more complete picture on the best way to build your particular box, prevent any difficulties in constructing or moving, and how to get the most out of your SFG with boxes that serve your particular gardening needs.

? Can I paint my box?

! Well, sure you can. Just as the long the paint stays on the outside of the box. You see, SFG is a totally natural and organic style of gardening, so you don't want the chemicals in paint mixing with your soil or making their way into anything you grow. For the same reason, you should **never use pressure-treated wood.** Be especially careful if you're looking to reclaim wood from any place other than a basic construction site. For instance, back in the 1970s, a lot of people used railroad ties to make raised beds. Problem was, those ties had been soaked in toxic creosote, which leached right out into the soil. That's why you also want to avoid wood left over from a deck-building project unless you're absolutely certain it hasn't been treated with preservatives. By and large, most Square Foot Gardeners I meet seem to prefer the natural beauty of wood for their boxes.

? Is there an easy way to spiff up the grids on my SFG boxes?

! That depends on what look you're after, but keep in mind that the grid has to be highly visible in any case—it's not an SFG without the grid. I usually suggest people buy wood strips called "lath" at their local home center or lumberyard. These thin strips already come in 4-foot lengths that you can buy for about a quarter each, so they're inexpensive and fit an SFG box perfectly. You can paint the top of the strips (don't paint any portion that comes in contact with your Mel's Mix) if you want to dress the box up a little bit. If you're willing to spend a little bit more money, you can buy lightweight vinyl grid strips off the Square Foot Gardening website (www.squarefootgardening.org). These strips are easy to clean, look great all the time, and can easily be stored over winter. You can even turn to materials like vinyl strips if that's a look you like—just so long as nothing leaches from the strips into the Mel's Mix.

Can I use the new "safer" treated lumber to build my SFG boxes?

Even though it does not contain CCA (the wood preservative used up until 2003 or so), I'm just not convinced this "safer" lumber is really safe. Because there are so many types of other wood—and other materials—you can use, I would not recommend using this wood.

Doesn't untreated wood rot too soon to be a good choice for my SFG box?

Regular, untreated wood breaks down in three to five years under most conditions. So what? In three to five years you can go find more FREE wood and make new sides. Better than having to rototill an area five times as large EVERY spring. There are lots of alternatives available for boxes. Redwood and cedar are expensive but long-lasting. Vinyl and composites are expensive but last practically forever. You can even use logs, bricks, or stones.

Is there an ideal height for a raised SFG box?

There is, and the height is critical to making raised boxes usable for special-needs gardeners. A sit-down SFG box, such as you might build for a person in a wheelchair, should be **30 inches from the ground** to the top of the box. If a box is to be used while standing, make it so the distance from the ground to the top of the box is about 36 inches. You might want to adjust this measurement slightly if the gardener is very tall or very short. A wonderful feature of the SFG boxes is that they can be built to accommodate any gardener, even those who get around with the help of a walker or a cane.

MEL'S TIP: THE MOVEABLE FEAST

Nobody's going to stop you if you feel like staking your SFG boxes in place. A lot of people prefer to figure out the layout and then leave the boxes where they are, year after year. But keep in mind that there are a lot of advantages to making your boxes portable. How to do that? Add plywood bottoms to any boxes you want to move. They're not that heavy and fit in a van or pickup easily. Here are a few things you can do with a portable box:

- Spruce up a poolside party, barbecue, or even a special outdoor event such as a birthday party, by positioning your boxes around a central gathering area.

- Move the boxes into the garage in the event of extreme weather, such as hailstorms. Be careful not to disturb your plants too much as you move the box.

- Take it to Grandma's house for a birthday gift, or to a newlywed couple's home as a one-of-a-kind wedding gift that keeps on giving.

- Bring it to your child's school for a stunning show-and-tell that will excite the children and may even lead to a schoolyard garden!

I'll bet with a little imagination and some family brainstorming you could make a very long impressive list. And what family fun that would be, complete with photos on Facebook.

MEL'S STORIES

SFG LOVES LUCY

When I was first starting out to promote SFG, I invented several products to use with the method. The very first one of these was called the "Green Machine," and was basically a series of 1-foot-square mulch mats with holes in them representing SFG seed placing—1, 4, 9, or 16. You laid the mats inside a wood frame laid right on top of your existing garden soil. It made for easy planting of your SFG. Remember, the first version of SFG used improved existing soil. By laying the mulch mats on the soil, you kept the weeds down and the plants you wanted grew up through the 1-inch-diameter holes in the mat.

The mats also helped the temperature of the soil stay more uniform, and helped keep the soil in place during a heavy rainstorm or even a hailstorm. It had the added advantage of protecting sprawling crops like strawberries. Strawberries just lying on the dirt tend to ripen unevenly and can attract slugs and other bugs—so the Green Machine mats protected against that. The mats even came in different colors! (I keep telling myself I have to bring that product back . . . what do you think?) The frame and mats were designed to be easily packed up in a box for shipping, and we got orders from all over the country. Then one day, we got an order for two Green Machines from "Lucy Arnaz," at an address in Southern California. Well that got my attention, because Lucy Arnaz was better known by her stage name Lucille Ball, the comedienne of *I Love Lucy* fame! Well, you can imagine, we were pretty excited when we saw that order. It wasn't just that I was a big fan (because, honestly, I was), it was the potential of our first celebrity endorsement.

I started thinking, "We really ought to do something with this." So we put a short letter in the box with the Green Machines, asking her if we she might get back to us and let us know if we could at least use her name in promoting the Green Machine. Unfortunately, we never heard back from her, but I sure would have loved to have some pictures of Lucille Ball with the Green Machine—a big star getting out in her yard to do some Square Foot Gardening!

? I have several SFG boxes and I'd rather not pay for landscape fabric if I don't have to. Can't I just use a layer of newspaper or even cardboard under my box?

! I wish I could say yes because I like nothing better than saving money with an SFG, but newspapers are just too darn thin to hold back all the weeds that want to get to your delicious Mel's Mix. They'll grow right through it. As for cardboard, I originally felt that this was a great solution—easy, money-saving, and great for the environment. But at the Square Foot Gardening Foundation, we're always testing and learning, and we found that that over time, cardboard breaks down and actually adds some nice nutrients to the weed seeds underneath. Long about your second or third year, you'll have weeds sprouting like crazy in your SFG boxes.

An interesting sidenote on cardboard: After my first book (which said you can use cardboard) had been out for awhile, a competitive method also said cardboard was okay. So it was one of those copycat things. When our research showed it doesn't work, we changed it immediately, but I don't think the other method changed theirs. So if you use cardboard, you're going to have a lot of weeds after the first year. Getting rid of them is an awful lot of work nobody should have to do, so we head off that problem by insisting that gardeners **use quality landscaping fabric** under their boxes. Not the cheapest weed cloth or even black plastic garbage bags like some other garden methods suggest, but the best commercial-grade landscape weed fabric.

Can I use plywood sheets I found on a construction site as the bottom for my box?

That's a great idea! Just make absolutely sure that the plywood has not been treated with any preservatives or other chemicals or used to form concrete walls and you'll be good to go. Keep in mind that smaller SFG boxes—any with less than a 3-foot span—can use ⅜-inch plywood on the bottom. Regular 4 × 4 SFG boxes need sturdier ½-inch plywood. Definitely go with the ¾-inch if you plan on moving your 4 × 4 box quite a bit. Securely screw the plywood to all the side boards from the bottom, using at least four to six deck screws per side.

Does my box have to be made out of wood?

Heck no. As long as the material won't leach anything harmful into your Mel's Mix, you can **use whatever works** for you. Some Square Foot Gardeners build with scraps of the lightweight, durable, and attractive composite materials used in modern decking (as long as the manufacturer says it's okay for gardens). We have a picture on our website of some boxes an unauthorized manufacturer made out of the metal strips that are used for guard barriers alongside highways. We have even used brick, cinderblock, and stone, but some experts say the cinder blocks can leach contaminants into the garden soil, so I honestly don't know about that. Needs more study. Just my two cents here—I've always made my boxes out of wood, because it's so easy to work with and you can find lots of free lumber at construction sites.

❓ I would like to make a box just for my children to garden. Is there anything I should change?

❗ You bet. When I was developing the SFG method, I actually measured the length of many people's reach to determine how far gardeners could comfortably reach into a box and still tend their plants. It was 2 feet in from all sides but, of course, those people were adults. When we at the SFG Foundation started putting Square Foot Gardens in schoolyards, we realized that children can't reach in as far, which is why I developed the "Square Yard" system. The boxes are **3 × 3 instead of 4 × 4**—which is the size you should use if your children will be regularly gardening in their own box. I strongly feel all children should have their own box to be responsible for.

Here is another idea. When I had my TV show on PBS each week, I built a 3 × 3 with a plywood bottom for one of my granddaughters who was only 3 then. We just added sand and she had a sandbox placed right in the patio where her grandfather had his SFG boxes. She was delighted to spend many happy hours there right in the family patio garden. But then, one day she looked up and said "Poppy, when can I have my own garden box?" Well, what an easy thing to do, scoop out the sand with a dust pan and replace it with Mel's Mix and a 3 × 3 grid. It's called Family Gardening, and it is a far cry from my mother's garden, which I had to labor in all spring turning over her single row garden soil. And worse yet, I spent all summer hoeing all the weeds in the aisles. I hated that so much that when I left to go to college (Georgia Tech in Atlanta), I swore I would never garden again for the rest of my life! Be careful of what you wish for!

❓ What's the best way to protect my SFG from all the deer in my area?

❗ Seems like the more you consider the small footprint of an SFG, the more reasons you'll find to love it. That small size makes it easy to protect your garden from hungry deer (and raccoons and possums and . . .). Simply build a small 4-foot square cage of 1-inch chicken wire (the building centers all call it "poultry netting" now). Bend the wire fabric into a cube and tie it at the edges with heavy-duty twist ties. (Check out the illustration below to see what the finished cage looks like.) Place the cage over your plants to keep deer from making a meal of the vegetation. Remove the cage whenever you need to harvest or work on one of the squares. It's easy as punch and you can build the cage any size to suit what you're growing. But if the cage is more work than you want to do, you can buy netting to drape over your plants. The netting feels like cobwebs when the deer stick their nose in. I guess the feeling of cobwebs on your nose is pretty creepy, because deer plain don't like it and will turn down a free meal to avoid the netting. You can find deer netting at most garden centers and large home improvement stores.

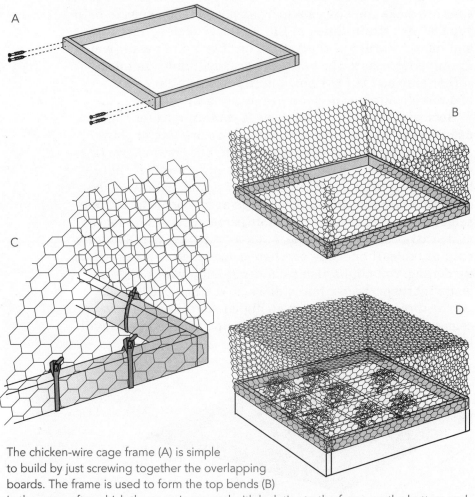

The chicken-wire cage frame (A) is simple to build by just screwing together the overlapping boards. The frame is used to form the top bends (B) in the cage, after which the cage is secured with lock ties to the frame on the bottom and along the corner seams (C). The finished frame (D) sits flush on top of the SFG box and protects the plants against damage, pets, and wildlife alike.

? I'm thinking of building an elevated SFG box to take advantage of a sunny spot on my patio. How can I make sure it's a success?

! Obviously you'll have to **put a bottom on your box,** and the material you use will be important in maintaining the integrity of the box. You didn't say whether you were mounting it on a table, so I'll assume you're either using legs or sawhorses. In either case, I recommend ⅝-inch plywood for a 3-foot space, and ½-inch plywood for a 4-foot space to make the box as sturdy as possible. Be sure to **drill your ¼-inch drain holes** in the center of each square foot and in each corner of the bottom or, if you don't want water draining right onto the patio surface, drill holes in one corner only and tilt the box slightly toward that corner—and put a container underneath to catch the water.

However, Mel's Mix is so good at retaining water that you usually won't have a lot of runoff. There are lots of ways to **build supports for your raised box,** but just be sure to make it sturdy, because you can be in big trouble if that box breaks or tips over on someone. I prefer to buy a used strong metal table with fold-up legs at my local thrift shop, something like a banquet table. It is much safer and leaves some extra room on the side. A 3 × 4 or a 4 × 4 will fit nicely on that table. If one side overhangs, even better for sit-down gardening. You might also consider raising your boxes up just slightly on bricks laid sideways. You can even stack two or three together. If you go higher, use cinderblocks or cement blocks. They can be on their side or on end and will be sturdy enough.

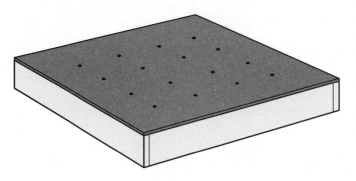

Drilling drainage holes in the plywood of an SFG box with a bottom is key to ensuring plant roots—and the bottom of the box—don't rot.

I'm moving and I'd like to take my SFG boxes with me. What's the best way to transport them?

All depends if you followed the original instructions for building your SFG box. You should be able to just **scoop the soil out into 5-gallon plastic pails** (you can usually get these FREE from local restaurants that are more than happy to get rid of them), pick up the weed barrier that sits underneath your Mel's Mix (you did remember to put down a weed barrier, right?) and then **put the SFG box right in the moving van** or, you can disassemble it and move the parts. Once you get to your new house, decide on the perfect place for your box, set it in position, lay the weed barrier down, and add the soil, then the grid. And BAM, you're all done. Easy as pie!

If you originally put a bottom on your box, then you just need to pick up the box with the help of a friend, and put it into the moving van! Soil and all. Stack several and brace them so that they don't shift in travel. Why, I have even known people who loaded fully planted SFG patio boxes on a truck for a 450-mile ride to another state. Can you imagine what those veggies said when they were unloaded? Ask the family!

? I'm not very handy. What is the easiest way to build a basic 4 × 4 SFG box?

! Don't worry, you're not alone. Many gardeners don't have well-developed do-it-yourself skills or even the tools necessary . . . and they don't need them for SFG. The easiest way to make a box is to go to your local lumberyard or home center and buy two 2 × 6 boards in standard 8-foot lengths (whichever wood you prefer or can afford, as long as it's not treated). Then ask the person who helps you to cut the wood exactly in half, and you'll have 4-foot lengths ready to be assembled into a box. From there, just take the wood home and drill the corners for 3 screws each corner (or nail them if you prefer, although screws are much stronger) and screw them together.

To use the boards as they are, you'll need to "rotate the corners," so that each successive board overlaps the previous as shown in the illustration. Now lay down a strong weed fabric in the base of the box and you're ready to fill it with Mel's Mix. Add a grid made from six pieces of wood lath you also can get at any lumber store. That's all there is to it!

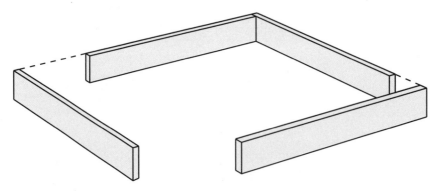

By overlapping each successive corner, we can simply cut all the sides to the same 4-foot length.

How much yield will I get from one box?

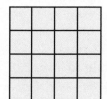 SFGs give you five times as much harvest from the same garden area as a single-row garden would. A 4 × 4 box will produce a dinner-sized salad every day during the growing season for one person. If you're setting a table for two, you'll want to grow two SFG boxes. Want dinner vegetables as well? Add an extra 4 × 4 box per person. Then, if you want some extra to can or freeze, consider adding an extra 4 × 4 box per person. So you have a choice per person of a basic 4 × 4 and an advanced 4 × 8, and an extravagant 4 × 12. A few or all can have a vertical frame for all those tomatoes, cucumbers, and squash you will want. Same rules apply to children, only their boxes will of course be multiples of 3 × 3. If you're still a little unsure, start small with one or two 4 × 4 boxes per person the first season (say spring). Then add season (summer) by season (fall) as you see how your harvest is working out.

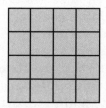 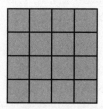

Determine the number of SFG boxes you will build and plant by how much harvest you'll really use.

How can I spruce up the aisles around my SFG boxes? They're just bare dirt now.

I hope you have a while to read this, because there are a whole lot of ways people make those aisles a part of their garden design. Once upon a time, I used single 12-inch-wide wood planks for my aisles, which mellowed to a nice natural color. But they were too narrow and we now recommend 3-foot aisles. The new, wider aisles create even more possibilities. If you're putting your garden out in a grassy area, it's just as easy to leave the grass in the aisles there. It's simple enough to mow as you normally would—the wide aisles leave plenty of room to run a mower through.

However, it sounds like the area you've chosen is bare dirt, which is really just a bare canvas for your creativity! You must lay down some of that thick, landscape fabric you'll find at nurseries or in the garden sections of most home centers. Get the best, most expensive (don't worry, it is the least expensive thing in your garden, but it will stop weeds cold for many years if you buy a good kind). The fabric is easy to use, looks nice, and blocks weeds. You could just walk on that but most everyone wants to cover it with something that looks nice and feels good under the feet.

I think a good place to start in any case is asking what type of material you can afford, is easy to walk on, comfortable to kneel on, good-looking, goes with the appearance of the rest of your yard, and will be easy to maintain. **Crushed stone** comes in lots of different sizes and colors (although make sure it's the rounded crushed stone, rather than the jagged type which will punch through your weed fabric). **Coarse or fine mulch** can do the trick, and there are lots of different looks depending on what was ground up to make the mulch. I've even seen gardeners layer their aisles with **dried grass clippings**, which create a thick, weed-defying mat, and are a great way to recycle yard waste that might otherwise overwhelm your compost pile with green material (just be sure to thoroughly dry the grass first or you'll have a mat of smelly, moldy, decaying material). If you want to go a little bonkers, by all means pave your aisles with **brick or stone pavers**, but I'd caution against going wild, especially in your first year—you may decide to reposition or reconfigure your boxes.

All that said, one of the best materials I've used is artificial turf. You can ask an artificial turf company for the cut pieces they can't otherwise use and you might get them for a song, or even free. Even if you don't have a local company, your local home center usually has big rolls of artificial turf. Have them cut you strips for your aisles and you'll probably be surprised by how cheap they are. The material doesn't need watering, mowing, or care of any kind and it stays green all year long. Best of all, the surface looks great!

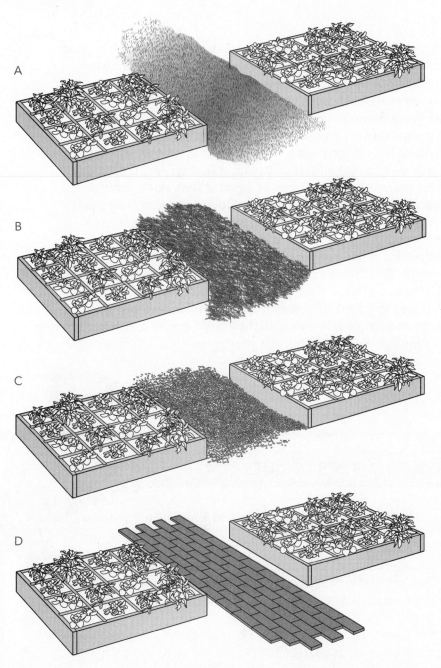

There are many paving options for the aisles between your boxes. Grass (A) is lovely underfoot but needs regular mowing; mulch (B) is easy to lay (put it over a barrier of weed fabric); crushed stone (C) can look very elegant and makes your boxes look neat and trim, and pavers (D) are a lot of work but you can't beat the upscale look!

Can I make smaller aisles to accommodate more boxes in my tiny backyard?

Can you? **Of course.** You'll still be able to reach in and work in the squares. The real question is, though, should you? When I first invented SFG, I laid down 12-inch-wide planks as walkways between my boxes. I managed to work in the garden, but it wasn't always easy and comfortable. That's why, when I was developing the improvements for my *ALL NEW Square Foot Gardening* book, one of the key changes was to make aisles at least 3 feet wide. I'd strongly suggest you make your aisles **at least 2 feet wide**, and if you can lay a few pieces of lumber down, see if you can walk and work and kneel in those two feet. If you find it a little tight then I'd suggest you'd make it a little wider. Three feet is perfect for most people, but if you want to narrow it down a little bit, feel free to do that, but practice first. It's hard to move the boxes after they're installed and planted.

Although my first SFG was mighty efficient with its 12-inch-wide aisles, it was a little too efficient, if you know what I mean.

MEL'S STORIES

I consider myself a pretty lucky guy because I've had lots of chances to see how SFG changes lives for the better. One of the most heartwarming cases I ever saw was a box we built on the roof of a hospital. We were able to put the box on a gurney and wheel it down to the room of a bedridden veteran. It gave him the chance to garden right from his bed and we could wheel it back up to the roof to get the sun it needed. There are so many great things you can achieve with portable SFG boxes that I'd urge you to consider making yours portable. If it would help in your situation to raise it up or down, or even wheel or carry it about, do it.

? Do I need to have a box? Why not one of the methods that uses just sloping sides of dirt or soil?

! That is a sloppy method with no definitive spacing or organization. Besides, sides that are just dirt wash down, get sloppy and irregular, and encourage a casual edge that invites a foot to walk into it. And besides all that, I think you'll like the organized appearance of the straight, well-defined sides. It encourages organization and efficiency so that we don't waste space, water, and all our natural resources in this environment.

? You say it's easy, but I don't know how to build anything and I don't have any tools.

! No tools? No skills? No problem. You can **buy prefab boxes** at many large home centers and retailers. The sides of the boxes just slip together. Others fit together and you just screw in the included hardware. But I would like to put in a plug for the boxes sold on the Square Foot Gardening website. They are made in the USA, with the box sides all cut out and slipped together, so no tools are required. Plus, all of the proceeds go to our non-profit foundation for all of our educational and humanitarian projects.

The tongue-and-pin box corner makes assembling your prefab SFG box as easy as can be.

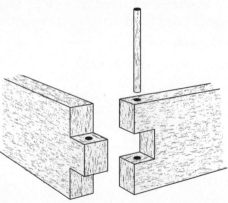

? I'd like a different look for my SFG; can I do without the grid and just organize my plantings in informal squares?

! If you'd like a different look, then you need a grid on your boxes. Embrace the grid! The grid is really the heart and soul of SFG. It's all well and fine to say that you'll keep the box organized in squares without it, but why try? In fact, an SFG without a grid is not really a Square Foot Garden. The beauty of the grid on top of the box is that it organizes everything for you so that you know what you've planted where.

Believe me, I've seen people try to work without the grid and the garden eventually gets out of hand. That's why, in developing the improvements for the *ALL NEW Square Foot Gardening*, I formalized the grid. We did away with strings and nails that could break and rust, and went to a sturdy, prominent wood grid. You can also use vinyl strips—find old blinds at a thrift store and you'll be able to buy all you need for $1! You may even find blinds in colors that will really jazz up your SFG box. Just cut the strings that hold the individual slats together and drill holes every 12 inches. Then use tiny nuts and bolts or brass "library pins" (you can find them at stationary stores) to hold the slats together in a permanent grid that will never rot and is easy to clean.

If you want to personalize your box or make it look a little different, you might want to paint or stain the grid (just not the underside that comes in contact with your Mel's Mix). You can also use a more unusual material, such as thick wood dowels or ½-inch PVC pipe for an entirely unique look. But **the grid really is essential** because it's the trademark of an SFG, and you can tell even from a distance that the grid is there and a Square Foot Garden is right underneath it. You should display it proudly for all it represents.

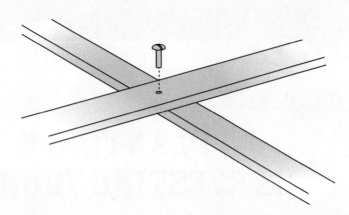

Pre-made grids include pins that hold the grid together and make it foldable for easy storage. It's not hard to make your own version with store-bought pins.

? Can I use string or twine for my grid?

! NO! I know the first book back in 1981 said you could, but after a lot of experience with strings getting dirty and breaking and being moved by growing plants, I realized we needed to have a stronger, more durable and more visible grid. I also found that when the string broke, it hardly ever got replaced, so you end up with a no-grid garden, and that's not a Square Foot Garden in its truest sense. There is a reason for each of the design principles and planting methods.

CHAPTER 3

PLANTING & HARVESTING YOUR SFG

The SFG method of gardening is focused on the plants. Everything we do, from giving them exactly the right amount of space between, to setting them in absolutely perfect soil, to giving them vertical supports that get them up off the ground and away from pests and disease, to giving them just the right amount of warmed water, is all about treating plants almost like pets. We pamper our garden. The result is a bountiful, healthy harvest with little work. What could be better than that?

"Why is that?" you might ask. Well, it's because if you treat your plants well, you'll be rewarded with a continuous supply of healthy and delicious produce. I call that one heck of a bargain. And let's not forget that tending your plants can be a rich life experience that reduces stress and gets you back into nature.

I've broken down planting and harvesting of your SFG crops—like all the other elements of SFG—into simple, commonsense practices. The idea, as always, is to minimize work, maximize plant health, and make tending your SFG an enjoyable experience. Although the things you need to know to grow healthy crops are all easy to understand, you're still going to have a few variables to consider as you go along. These will become just everyday decisions you make that seem just fun to do and have an air of excitement about them. Sort of like where should we go on vacation this year? What type of vegetables should you plant, and what other types of plants should you include? Which plants work best together? How will you get the most from your plants? Those are just some of the many questions we receive at the SFG Foundation, and they are just the tip of the iceberg.

This chapter will answer those questions and completely demystify the

"SFG is by far the BEST METHOD for someone who wants good veggies with the least amount of work."

—Leon from New Mexico

whole process of getting your crop from seed to mature plant in as little time, and with as little effort and resources, as possible. But along the way, I'll also provide some advice on how to make the more personal decisions that go into growing your plants. For instance, is it better to choose a high yield of something your family is less likely to love and eat, or pick a less prolific plant that produces a family favorite?

In any case, read through these questions and I think you'll find some eye-openers that will help you in your garden. Remember, do it right, do it according to the book (the system works, 2 million book buyers and followers can't be wrong can they?), and your SFG should provide you with a continual harvest from early spring right on through late fall (and maybe even beyond!).

MEL'S TIP: CHEERS!

Plants like beer! Don't just dump beer left in bottles after a party. Once it becomes flat—after a day or two—add the beer to your SFG bucket of sun-warmed water. The nutrients and salts in the beer will give your plants an added boost. Of course, if the dog seems a little dopey for no apparent reason, you'll know you need to put a cover on that bucket!

How do I get asparagus to grow in my SFG?

I've found that the secret to growing asparagus is a little like the best way to deal with children—**lots and lots of patience**. You see, asparagus is a biennial that takes a few years of becoming established before it will yield its first harvest. If you're like most people, you're going to want a lot of asparagus when it finally comes time to harvest. That's why I recommend planting an entire 4 × 4 SFG box entirely with asparagus. Traditionally, we recommended one plant per square foot, but I've found that if you can afford enough of the rootstock, planting four per square foot will give you a much bigger crop earlier. Planting them, however, is a little different than planting a vegetable from seed or transplant. You'll buy 2- or 3-year-old rootstock from a nursery or a mail order outlet and you have to plant it a special way. Fill the box with about 3 inches of Mel's Mix and make little mounds at each spot you'll be placing a plant (one to four per square foot, depending on your budget). Then drape the roots over each mound. Finally, pour in the remaining 3 inches of Mel's Mix to the top of the box covering the roots an inch or two.

Here's a little advice to make things easier for you. Always leave a generous aisle around SFG boxes planted with asparagus because the plants grow quite bushy and like a lot of room to spread out. I'd also be real careful where you place the box because those plants can last up to two decades! After the spring harvest of spears is done, let the plants grow and get bushy to gain strength for next year (but you can snip off a few feathery top leaves as filler in flower arrangements).

What kind of flowers should I plant in my SFG to attract birds into the yard?

That's a good question. Although some birds look to steal your harvest—crows, blue jays, and robins, to name a few of the worst thieves—many birds will feed on insects that could damage your crops. They are also just nice to look at and listen to; I think songbirds really add a lot to any garden, and certainly to your SFG. Here are some flowers to consider, and the birds they attract. Keep in mind that most of these also make stunning cut-flower arrangements.

Purple Coneflower: Hummingbirds and goldfinches

Zinnia: Juncos, white-crowned sparrows

Cosmos: Sparrow, juncos

Sunflower: Indigo bunting, sparrow

Bachelor's Button: Tufted titmouse, cardinal

Zinnias are bird favorites that beautify your SFG box and provide the bonus of cut flowers for display all summer long.

I don't understand how I can fit one tomato plant per square when they grow to be so bushy?

The trick is that, in SFG, we grow all vine tomatoes vertically, **pruning off the side suckers** that would eventually grow into side branches and take a lot of energy from the main plant. The side branches are what make a tomato spread out. By removing them, we keep the energy in the main stem, which makes for a thinner, more productive plant and larger fruit! The other variety of tomato plants don't grow tall as a vine but squat as a bush. They are called determinate, while the vine types are called indeterminate. That's expert lingo for "I can determine how tall the bush variety will get (it says so on the tag), but I cannot determine how tall the vine varieties will get because they just keep growing taller and taller until frost kills them." Of course that's why we **provide strong, sturdy, tall supports** for our tomatoes and not stakes or cages. That's what the tomato tower is for. A 4 foot wide by 6 foot high tower will accommodate four vine type tomato plants. And it's so easy you just weave them in and out of the netting. Determinate and indeterminate translates into SFG lingo as bush versus vine.

What kind of plants will attract butterflies to my SFG?

Butterflies just love flowers. That's their drinking fountain full of the nectar they feed on. So you'll want to add some flowers to your SFG box if you want these pretty insects to pay a visit. Here are some of butterflies' very favorite flowers: Daisy, zinnia, cosmos, marigold, Black-eyed Susan, purple coneflower, and violets.

I know Mel's Mix contains no weed seeds, but what if a bird drops weed seeds or they blow over from a neighbor's yard?

First of all, you'll be able to see the odd weed very quickly and clearly because it will grow outside the established patterns of 1, 4, 9, or 16 that you planted your seeds in. Here's the best part though: because Mel's Mix is so loose and friable, you just pluck that weed with two fingers. You've never walked on the soil so the weed's roots will pull right out. Think back now to row gardening where you are continually chopping the weeds down with your trusty hoe. All you are really doing is chopping off the top of all the weeds because the ground is so tough and compacted from walking on it. Then the weed root just sprouts again as soon as you run your sprinkler or stand there watering your big row garden with a hose. Then you have to come back again in four weeks to start all over again. Just one of the subtleties of SFG.

When should I plant my warm-weather vegetables?

When the weather gets warm! No, I'm kidding. I was just being playful. Now for the correct and useful answer. I know someone who knows the exact answer and is right in your neighborhood. Start planting after the last frost date for your area. You can determine that date by contacting your local Cooperative Extension Service office, or check online—there are many different sources listing the frost dates for regions across the country. That's all you have to do. Get that first frost date for your location. Then, open your *ALL NEW SFG* book and **follow the planting chart.** It tells you when to plant seeds either indoors or outdoors and when to plant transplants outdoors. It even tells you when you can expect to start harvesting and, finally, how long the harvest will last. How's that for a lot of info in one page? It's all in the magic of charts and diagrams and you know, as an engineer, I love charts for all this info. Good luck with your summer crop.

? I don't want to plant seeds that might not sprout. How do I avoid that?

! If that's a big concern with you, and you've got a lot of money and don't want to take a chance, or if your seeds have been around a couple of years, then I'd say **buy fresh seeds every year** rather than saving seeds in the refrigerator like I recommend. Over time, saved seeds will slowly (very slowly) degenerate and the rate of germination will go down. You can plant a larger pinch if your seeds are getting old—say, four or five seeds rather than two or three—to ensure some come up. But be careful about planting too many seeds. You don't want to spend a lot of time snipping seedlings, and overplanting is one of the reasons row gardening is not as efficient as SFG.

? Do you advocate soaking seeds before planting?

! I'm not religious about soaking seeds and I don't think it's worthwhile in most cases, especially small, hard-to-handle seeds. However, I do **soak larger seeds**, such as bean, corn, cucumber, squash, and pea seeds, for 15 to 20 minutes before planting. Those are the ones that the birds like, so a presoaking will get your seeds off to a fast start.

These are pea seeds, but any large seeds can benefit from a brief soak. Soak them in a tray or cup and take note: any seeds that float are not viable and won't produce a plant—discard them.

? I'm having trouble deciding exactly which vegetables to plant in my SFG. Any suggestions?

! It's not hard: the best vegetables are the ones **you like the most and that will produce the most food for you.** How hard is that? If you have a little experience in gardening, plant the vegetables that have grown well for you in the past. If you mean the best varieties of, say, cabbage or carrots, well then read the seed catalog and pick those that sound good. Choosing what to plant is no more difficult than choosing what to order from the menu when you go out to eat. Of course your spouse might turn to you and say, "Honey, I don't know what I want, what should I order?" Then you will have to start asking a lot of questions to get close to what they should order. Gardening is no different than eating. You can always call your County Extension Agent for a list of recommended varieties to plant in your area.

? Is it okay to use chemical fertilizers and supplements in my SFG boxes?

! No! **Absolutely NOT.** I spent a lot of time thinking about and testing the Mel's Mix formula to give plants just the right blend of nutrients. You don't need to spend extra money on commercial soil supplements—that's one of the big benefits of including five different types of compost and adding your own homemade compost each time you replant. Also, the nutrients your plants get from compost are natural, organic and won't burn the plant like many commercial formulas will.

? I understand why I should water carefully by hand, but why does the water need to be sun-warmed?

! Ever take a cold shower? Your plants don't like a shock either. **Warm water is easier for roots to take up,** and it doesn't take much effort to have a pail alongside each SFG box. That sun provides FREE energy.

? Do I have to rotate crops? It seems complicated to me.

! I like to think that nothing about SFG is complicated; I made it simple so you wouldn't have to worry about things like crop rotating, which is the process of switching from one plant family to another from year to year. But make no mistake, **easy crop rotation** is one of the many advantages of SFG over row gardening. That's because in SFG, crop rotation is just about automatic. Remember, that rule No. 10 is when you're done harvesting a square of plants, you add a handful of compost, and replant with a new and different crop. Usually, and this is the best part of SFG; the season is changing and you'll go from a cool-weather crop (say, radishes) in the spring, to a warm-weather crop in the summer (say, bush beans), back to a cool-weather crop in the fall (say, spinach). Guess what you have just done and didn't even know it? Crop rotation! You started with a root crop, changed to a fruiting crop, and ended with a leaf crop.

Each crop requires different nutrients, space, and growing conditions. And, you didn't even have to take a college course, study complicated procedures, or learn big horticultural words. When it's time to decide, you just look around and think, "What would I like more of next, and what season is it?" That's the simplicity of SFG and that's why so many beginners say, "I can do that!" Some people like to keep elaborate records, even on their computer; others just look at their garden and know right away what they need.

? Can I grow fruit like raspberries, blackberries, or blueberries in my SFG?

! Growing berries in an SFG isn't a problem; the difficulty lies in keeping them from spreading where you don't want them. That's why **we generally don't plant berries**—especially invasive blackberries and raspberries. They just like to take over! Most berry plants spread underground through their root system and pop up, usually in the last place you want them to.

If you absolutely must have your berries, plant them in Mel's Mix as you would any other plant, but confine them to their very own long, narrow box (2 feet wide by however long you wish). Plant only the berry plants, one per square foot. Blackberries in particular prefer to sprawl out along the ground, so plan to tie the canes to a support. Raspberries are more upright and won't need it. Blueberries are the hardest to grow and require a specific climate to thrive, so contact a large local nursery or your local Cooperative Extension Service agent for suggestions and advice growing blueberries where you live. They also prefer acidic soil, somewhere in the range 4 to 4.5 pH—Mel's Mix is normally just about neutral at 7 pH.

To give your blueberries a fighting chance, you'll need to add more peat moss to the mix and use a test kit to test the pH regularly so that you maintain the correct acidity. No matter which berries you grow, add more compost to the soil each year to replenish the nutrients.

? What type of gloves do you recommend for working in an SFG?

! I think the only gloves you need are the ones made out of skin that you were born with. I use gloves when I'm working with wood because splinters can be nasty, but when I'm gardening, I think it's important to feel the soil, caress

Continued

your flowers, and handle your vegetables. Part of the joy of gardening is the contact you have with your plants. Gloves get in the way of that. If you don't want your fingernails to get dirty, scrape them on a bar of soft soap before going to the garden. That will sort of plug them up from dirt entering underneath them, which makes wash-up easy.

MEL'S TIP

Pretty up a chain-link fence—or any fence for that matter—with a hanging SFG. We designed a wooden box for our SFG online store that was 6 inches wide × 6 inches deep, and 1, 2, 3, and 4 feet long to dress up a fence. Hang it from a chain-link fence with holes drilled in the back of the box near the top and slip in S hooks which then just hook on the fence. Be sure to drill drainage holes in the bottom, and consider planting trailing plants like cucumbers, and vining plants like tomatoes, which will look lovely in the boxes. You could also add a few flowers to really make the fence look great.

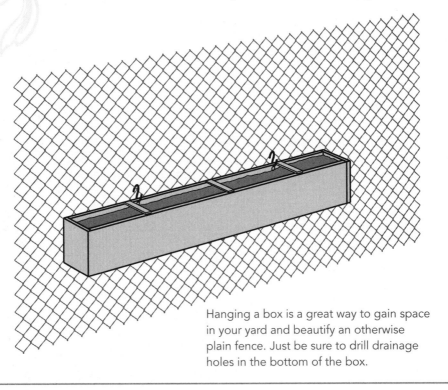

Hanging a box is a great way to gain space in your yard and beautify an otherwise plain fence. Just be sure to drill drainage holes in the bottom of the box.

What's the best way to harvest leaf lettuce?

! Use the **children's scissors** you keep by your SFG box (you did buy the children's scissors I recommended, right?), and regularly cut off the large outer leaves, leaving the lighter, smaller inner leaves. The plant will continually produce until the weather gets too hot. You'll know the season is over when the lettuce becomes bitter and "bolts"—or sends up a seed stalk. Another reason why this cool weather plant is so excellent for a fall garden, it will never bolt and you can harvest it right up until winter.

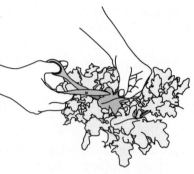

Use your scissors to cut the larger outer lettuce greens every time you want a salad.

MEL'S STORIES

A TREE IN MY SFG

Every so often, I have someone ask me if it's possible to grow a tree in their SFG box. I don't know why they would want to. Trees take up a lot of space, they need to send their roots far out and down deep into the soil, and they shade all the other plants around them. So you'd have to be talking about a very small, very skinny tree, or something like an ornamental specimen—which wouldn't add much in terms of produce to the garden. But because I experiment with most everything at one time or another, I did once grow a dwarf fruit tree in a 3 × 3 SFG box. I planted it in the center and then planted the outer squares, all eight of them, with strawberries, four per square foot. The strawberries did well, and so did the fruit tree, but I don't think it got all it needed from the Mel's Mix—it probably spread its roots a little farther down than that. It looked lovely and was one of my more unusual SFG boxes. Just the same, I don't think an SFG box is the place for a tree.

How long should I let the drip irrigation in my SFG run?

That's like asking how long to let the hose run to fill up my swimming pool. It depends on your rate of flow of course, but generally between 15 minutes and 1 hour. But let me get up on my soapbox here for a second, now that you bring it up. I'm not opposed to drip irrigation systems for SFG. I understand some people are very busy, and I appreciate gardeners who want to make sure that their plants get the water they need.

Drip irrigation can also be a great way to conserve water. I just have two problems with it. First, **the water needs of your plants are going to be different at different times**. A big bushy pepper plant needs a whole lot more water than a seedling does. If the weather has been windy and hot recently, your SFG beds are going to need significantly more moisture than they usually do. Most drip irrigation systems I've seen don't automatically account for these types of variables. And if you're not watering your plants by hand every day, it's easy to miss when they become parched. Second, I think drip irrigation is a less satisfying alternative to watering the plants by hand.

Keeping a sun-warmed bucket of water next to your SFG box is a great way to make sure you can water any time you think your plants need it. And when you water by hand, you touch, caress, and interact with your plants, which is one of the nicest things about gardening. It also gives you a chance to stick your finger down in the soil and check for certain if the plant needs water or not. There, now I'll step down off my soapbox! And now that I'm down, I want you to understand that I fully realize that anyone who has to be away from the house, like at school or work or travels, hand watering is not a good solution and drip is a great solution, especially with an automatic timer, but it separates you from your plants.

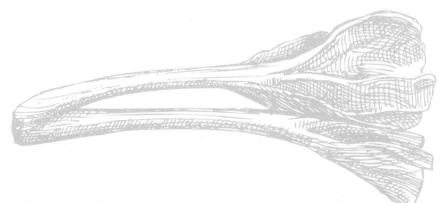

Any advice on growing roses in my SFG?

Sure. The problem with roses is that they tend to get pretty big and they need a lot of space. For the plant to stay healthy, air should circulate freely around the rose, and a mature rose's roots usually go deeper than 6 inches.

That's why, when I meet a rose lover who really wants roses in her SFG, I say, **"Go miniature!"** Miniature roses are compact enough for a single-square planting in your SFG box, and they are just beautiful. Matter of fact, when we filmed an episode of my PBS TV show in Disney World, I copied their English rose garden in miniature roses. You can find miniatures in almost all the colors of the rainbow and in long-blooming varieties.

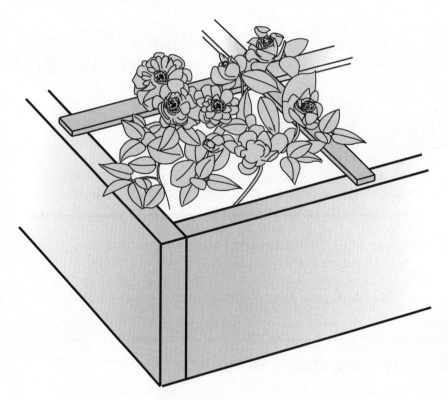

A miniature rose adds all the beauty and elegance—in far less space—of its larger cousins. It can be brought in for the winter, or left right in the box!

What extra steps should I take to protect my SFG box on very hot summer days?

Keep in mind that your plants are a little like children. When they are very hot and sweaty, you give them a drink. So in extreme heat, you'll want to **water your SFG plants more frequently**. You also move children into shade when they are overheated, right? You can do the same thing with the plants in your SFG boxes, by **draping shade cloth** over the PVC pipe frame described on page 22. You can also make sure moisture stays in the soil by adding several inches of mulch on top of your Mel's Mix.

Any recommendations of cut flowers to grow in my SFG?

The important thing here is you add a few flowers among your SFG squares. Cut flowers are extra nice additions because they not only look nice in the SFG box, they also pretty up the house when cut and displayed in a vase. I'm partial to the daisy family of flowers, but you should grow whatever flowers really tickle your eye or nose. Most any cut flower will do well in an SFG box, but **be careful with tall flowers**, such as some types of tall-growing zinnias; make sure you plant those on the north side (back) of the box so that they don't shade out your other plants. Other types get so big and bushy, that they are not good candidates for a SFG.

MEL'S TIP: GOOD PLANTS TO THE RESCUE!

Savory and chamomile are great additions to any garden. The first can be a wonderful salad green, and the second is excellent for making teas and tinctures. Both attract beneficial insects that will help pollinate all your plants. I'd suggest you consider planting these near your warm-weather summer blossoming varieties, such as peppers, eggplants, beans, tomatoes, and squash.

If you could only grow one crop in your SFG, what would it be?

That's a tough one. I'd have to say **leaf lettuce, green or red**. Easy to grow, you can harvest these greens all spring, summer with shade, and fall. Just keep replanting as each crop becomes finished and bolts to seed. All varieties taste great, are nutritious and I don't think I'd ever get tired of it!

SHELF LIFE OF YOUR HARVEST

There's just no controlling when your plants deliver their bounty. Your plants can produce more vegetables in some weeks than in others, so it's important to know what will last in the refrigerator, and what won't. Here's a list of common SFG harvest crops and their refrigerator lifespan.

HOW MANY DAYS DO SFG CROPS LAST IN THE REFRIGERATOR?

3 TO 4 DAYS	5 TO 6 DAYS	1 TO 2 WEEKS
Corn	Broccoli	Beets
Cucumbers	Cauliflower	Cabbage
Eggplant	Leeks	Carrots
Lettuce & Spinach	Peppers	Garlic
Beans	Tomatoes	
Squash	Melons	

What type of zucchini have you had good luck with in SFGs?

The short answer is, "the kind that climbs." Zucchini is a favorite summer squash that you can use in lots of different dishes, and a single plant will usually give you plenty of zucchini, especially when it has Mel's Mix to feed it. You can grow "bush" varieties of zucchini in your SFG, but they'll take up a lot of room—9 square feet for one bush! That's the space of a 3 × 3 box! Their leaves are big and zucchini bushes just love to sprawl out, often shading other plants and cheating them out of their fair share of the sun. That's why I developed a trick to growing zucchini.

Rather than struggle with keeping an unruly bush in line, **I grow vine varieties vertically** (usually, if the seed packet isn't labeled with the word "bush" you've got a vine variety). My trick is to plant the seed or seedling right in the center of 2 square feet either on the right or left side of the box but in the back of a 4 × 4 right next to your vertical frame. As the plant grows, carefully raise the end and weave it into the vertical support netting for your SFG. You're sure to discover the best part of growing zucchini this way—unlike sprawling bush or vine zucchini grown in a row garden (in which new fruit and blossoms primarily grow at the end, leaving the base stem and leaves ugly and withered), a vertically trained zucchini plant grows a greater number of fruit and looks much nicer over time.

You'll have to pay attention as your zucchini plant gets going, because it will still want to lie down. Keep lifting the end and weaving it into the netting at least once every week, and you'll soon have a beautiful tree of zucchini!

Which work better in SFGs: seeds or transplants?

Both will grow just fine in your SFG, so the question is really, "Which is better for you?" If you want to save some money and you don't mind being a little more patient, I'd go with seeds. If you're planting late or don't want to wait for the seeds to sprout, or not sure it will sprout or grow—and you don't mind a significantly higher cost—buying a transplant at the store will fill the bill and there is no waiting or wondering if it will be a healthy plant. You get to pick it out from all the others. I guess someone could say that would be like do you want to have a baby by planting a seed or just go to the nursery and pick a young one out to take home. Now THAT is going to cause a lot of discussion I know. I don't mean for a moment any slant or opinion or agenda so please don't write me a letter saying, "How could you compare?"

If I accidentally pull out a plant when harvesting or weeding my vegetables, have I killed it?

Not by a long shot. **You just pop that plant right back in** its hole, firm around it, and give it a bit of shade and water. It will come right back to full health. (You'll probably be more shocked than that plant was!) By the way, knowing how to harvest is very important. I got a letter once from a lady who said, "I watched you on your Discovery Network TV show and you just grabbed a tomato, twisted it, and pulled it right out." I tried to harvest a pepper the same way and I pulled the whole plant out." That's funny but true, so in my SFG cookbook I tell readers how to best harvest every vegetable and herb for that very reason.

What is the most unusual thing you've ever seen growing in an SFG?

Baby rabbits! A viewer sent us photos of a **mother rabbit** who had dug out one square of a box and proceeded to have her brood. There's a time to get rid of garden invaders, and then there's the times when you just have to accept them. The viewer just took a lot of pictures and waited for the youngsters to be old enough to go out on their own. And I'll bet she didn't put out a "For Rent" sign.

MEL'S TIP: DINNER PARTY IN THE GARDEN

There's no need to bring your salad makings to the table, when you can take your dinnerware right to the salad makings! When you're ready for a fresh vegetable salad, just take your salad bowl out to the garden and cut what you want right there (you did leave your SFG scissors next to the box, right?). This is a great way to get children interested in eating their greens and, in fact, I've met people who have parties and give everyone a bowl to go cut their own custom salad. Now that's having some SFG fun! Well, what about root crops like radishes and carrots, Mel? Well, why do you think we have a bucket of sun-warmed water right next to each box? A couple of swishes and pop that baby right in your mouth. You see, all the parts and components of SFG fit together and even interlock. It is a total system.

? Can I grow leeks in my SFG? They require a fairly swampy environment.

! You bet you can. The rule is the same as with other SFG crops: build up, not down. In the case of leeks (and some carrots and potatoes, as well), you'll need to provide the root crop with deeper soil. That means **building a 1-foot deep SFG box**. I recommend that when gardeners want to grow these specific crops, they build a special SFG square 1-foot × 1-foot × 6-inch box we call a "top hat" for just that crop. Then you put it right on top of an existing square and fill it with Mel's Mix. That way, you have 12 inches of soil and you can grow the crop without having to build your regular 4 × 4 SFG boxes a whole lot deeper. And be sure to give your leeks plenty of water.

? Any tips for planting seedlings or transplants in SFGs?

! First, we need to understand our terms. A seedling is a recently sprouted seed that has at least two pairs of leaves. The first is called the seed leaf and eventually falls off, the second pair and those above it are called true leaves. You can transplant a seedling anytime once that second set of true leaves has formed, and right up until a short bushy plant that has at least six sets of leaves, when we call that a "transplant." At least out here in the West, that's what we call it. Some folks on farms and in the New England area call them "starts."

I prefer seeds because they're so darn cheap, and they're easy to grow in an SFG (easier than in row gardens, that's for sure). But I also realize that some gardeners like to start their plants early, on a windowsill or under a grow light. Sometimes, you get a late start and need to buy your favorite plants from a nursery. That's okay; I made the SFG method to be adaptable, no matter what you're planting. However, you need to take a little more care with planting seedlings or

Continued

transplants, because they tend to be a bit more delicate than seeds. Start by soaking six-packs of seedlings or transplants in a bucket of sun-warmed water. If you've started a seed in a cup of vermiculite, it won't need to be soaked.

When you're ready to put your seedling in its new SFG home, make sure the soil in the square is thoroughly moist. Make a hole with a pencil and wiggle the pencil around to widen the opening so that you can comfortably fit the seedling's roots in the hole. Then sprinkle a little water in the hole. I'm a fan of loosening the rootball of a large potted transplant to make sure the plant isn't "rootbound" and to give it its best possible start. Set the transplant down in the hole you've made and carefully firm the soil around the new plant, making a little saucer-shaped depression around it for the water to get right to the roots.

Now here's an important part of the process that a lot of gardeners forget: give that transplant plenty of shade. You want to keep it from wilting too much and getting dried out. You'll also want to make sure it has plenty of water until it's well established.

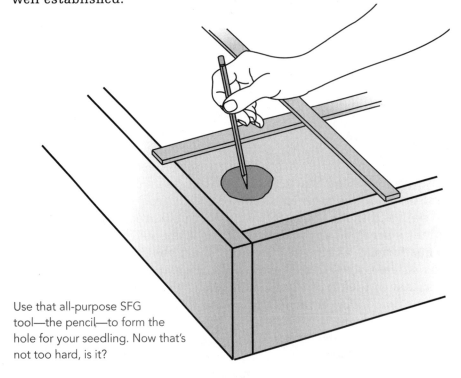

Use that all-purpose SFG tool—the pencil—to form the hole for your seedling. Now that's not too hard, is it?

❓ Is there any way I can keep my SFG lettuce from bolting in the mid summer?

❗ As you're finding out, lettuce is traditionally a cool-weather crop that will go to seed under a hot summer sun. That heat and sunlight signal to the plant that it's time to reproduce, which is why it stops making edible leaves and turns bitter and grows a seed head. Once it starts this process of "bolting," there's no stopping it. The trick is to keep your lettuce cool and shaded. That's pretty easy to do in the confines of an SFG box. Place some stakes into the corners of the square that holds the lettuce, then tie shade cloth so that it hangs over the plants. That will keep them out of the overwhelming sun.

To keep those plants cool, give them a lot of extra water. You can water more regularly and put a heavy layer of mulch down, and you might do what I do—keep a nice spray bottle full of water next to the box in its shade and give your lettuce a spritz every time you're in the garden. That should keep them growing salad greens for a little longer. Another idea is to start some other "heat resistant" or "summer tolerant" varieties of lettuce that have been bred to withstand hotter temperatures without bolting. Start these a couple of weeks before the early spring varieties seem to lose their vigor so you can have lettuce all year in every season. Then in late summer, plant tolerant or cold weather varieties for your fall and winter crop.

But remember rule No. 10: do not plant in the same square as your previous summer crop. We do crop rotation. Your seed catalog is your year-round friend for all the varieties available.

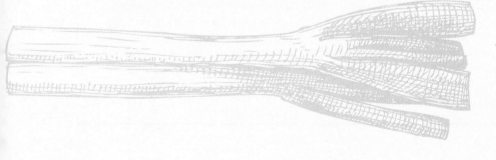

I prefer big tomatoes. Won't big tomato plants be stunted in an SFG?

Oh **goodness no**. I had a tomato plant in my vertical SFG that grew 28 feet high. After it topped the vertical support, I ran a thin rope right up into a tree and the tomato plant didn't stop until the first heavy frost. The largest individual tomato I've ever grown was almost the size of my granddaughter's head (and I have the photo to prove it!). Give your SFG tomatoes plenty of support, lots of nutrients from your Mel's Mix, and plenty of water, and they'll do the rest, believe me.

Tomatoes about the size of my granddaughter's head. Thanks to the SFG way of growing!

MEL'S TIP: POWER WATER FOR PLANTS

You know how people buy bottled vitamin water in the store? Well you do the same for your SFG plants! Enrich the water with extra calcium and minerals by dropping eggshells into your bucket of sun-warmed water. Leave them there for a couple of days and the nutrients from the shells will leach out into the water. Chopped-up dried banana peels will add essential potassium and phosphorous. A small amount of coffee grounds added to water will boost the nitrogen going to your plants, and will spur strong green growth. After you're finished with any of these ingredients, remove them, crunch up them up as necessary and add to the compost pile, or dig them right into your Mel's Mix.

How do I grow all the strawberries I want from my SFG?

There's nothing like fresh-picked strawberries and your SFG is just the place to grow them. If you're familiar with this favorite fruit, you'll know it spreads by way of "runners" that grow out across the soil and set down roots. You can plant just one strawberry plant per square foot, and let the runners propagate. However, I've found it simpler, quicker and more effective to plant four strawberries per square foot and clip the runners before they have a chance to set. That way, all the energy in the plant goes toward growing those delicious berries. Use my method and you can expect a harvest for as many as three and often up to five years. Now that's a return on your investment!

After a few years, when your harvest begins to dwindle, pull out and replace the plants. Or that year, let four of the runners from each plant set root in the soil and clip off any others. You can choose from three types for your SFG: June-bearing that grow fruit only in June (or what the plant thinks is June); everbearing, which fruit twice during the season, and "day neutral" strawberries that will grow fruit as long as the temperature stays above freezing and below 85°F.

Runners are a way for the strawberry to propagate, but in SFG we cut them back so that the plant focuses its energy on producing all that sweet, delicious fruit.

Nine bush beans per square foot? That just seems like an awful lot. Won't the bean plants crowd one another out?

I know people are a little surprised by some of the plant spacings when they first start Square Foot Gardening, but it's just a matter of mathematics and the recommended spacing from the seed company. Now, if you looked at a packet of bush bean seeds and the recommended spacing on the label were 12 inches, you'd only be planting one plant per square. If it were half that, 6 inches, you'd plant four per square (because there are four 6-inch squares in every square foot, right?). As it is, seed companies recommend spacing bush beans every 4 inches. That looks like a lot of space in a row, but tends to look a little cozier in one square of an SFG.

Just the same, we're giving the plant the recommended space—because there are nine 4-inch squares in a square foot! And I'll tell you, those bush beans like the company. When the plants leaf out, they shade the soil, slowing moisture loss from evaporation. Because they are fairly constrained on all sides but not crowded, the plants tend to put their energy in bean production rather than foliage production. I think you're going to be amazed, and very happy, at your first season's bounty of beans.

To make that spacing idea a little clearer, let me ask you something. If the bean plants in a row garden are supposed to be thinned to 4 inches apart, why does the next row have to be 3 feet away? And to make matters worse, 3 feet on each side of that single row? That's 6 feet of space in one direction, and 4 inches in the other direction. Do you see the absurdity of single row gardening? If the bean plant can be thinned to every 4 inches in a row, why can't the next row be 4 inches away? Instead, they are teaching it should be 3 feet away. When I ask an expert that question, he'll scratch his head, take off his cap, get a little flushed in the face, hem and haw a little, and finally say "Well, it just seems too close."

Have you ever tried it? "Well, no, but I just don't think it will work!"

Why not? "Well, we have never done it that way." That seems like a pretty good scientific reason, don't you think? I rest my case and will get off my soapbox. Thank you all for your attention.

? My watermelon vines are growing, but I'm not seeing any watermelons. Am I doing something wrong?

! You should have no problem growing watermelons—and other melons for that matter—in your SFG. You need a fairly long summer season, but Mel's Mix is the ideal foundation for watermelon. If your plants are not bearing fruit, it could be because of pollination. Most **melons need to be pollinated,** male blossom to female blossom, which is the one with a miniature melon at the base of the flower.

In rare cases where you're growing your SFG in a sheltered or otherwise protected area, or the weather is such that the insects, that visit the blossoms to get the nectar, can't get to them, you may need to take matters into your own hands. You can do this by simply picking a male blossom (the one without a miniature melon), strip or cut off the pedals and rub it inside the female blossom (the one with a little miniature melon at the base if its flower). Rub the two together so that the insides—where that sticky pollen is—are thoroughly in contact. If there are any kids around, you can use this as a birds-and-the-bees lesson, but I will leave that up to you. Just don't tell anyone that Mel told you this story. Please.

A little extra advice: Once your plants are properly pollinated, you'll need to prepare for those delicious, yet big, fruits to come. In SFG we grow melons vertically. Just like a tomato or squash plant, you weave the growing end in and out of that soft nylon netting weekly; it's a no-staking, no-tying method I have developed for easy gardening the SFG way. In the case of watermelons, grow the small varieties like "Sugar Baby" or you need to be darn sure your vertical frame is strong as all get out. Keep your netting tight and check the rebar supports regularly. But don't worry about the fruit stem holding the melon; the plant is designed to support the fruit no matter what.

> *"Your method has given me the confidence to try veggies again after a few feeble attempts."*
>
> —Anne from Florida

What if I want to grow more exotic plants that aren't covered in your book?

I love to see people experimenting with new crops and plants in their SFGs, but given all the possibilities it's almost impossible to provide complete and comprehensive yield and planting data in one place—especially since every region of the country has its own particular climate and horticultural variations. That's why the best way to get answers to specific planting questions that aren't covered in my books is to **contact your local Cooperative Extension Service agent**, or local university horticultural program. They have tons of information on local growing conditions, regional plants, pests and critters that are problems in your area, and much more. You can also do a general search on the Internet and find a lot of information that way—including personal stories from other gardeners in your area. (Although I would caution you to take the advice you find in online forums with a healthy grain of salt and always double-check it.)

As a beginner, are there certain crops I should avoid?

I like to start beginners out with **simpler crops** that they, and their families, will enjoy. Things like carrots, lettuce, radishes, and pansies are all pretty simple to grow in an SFG in the spring. For summer or warm-weather crops, stick with marigolds, beans, peppers, squash, and tomatoes. For a fall crop, go back to cool-weather crops like spinach, beets, green onions, and the same ones you grew in the spring, but also add the cabbage family. Other crops, such as corn, potatoes, watermelons, pumpkins, perennial flowers and spring bulbs take a little bit more space, extra care, and sometimes require special support. Anything that grows tall, such as corn, or climbs may need support and attention in an SFG. I would stay away from those plants in your first year. Just get used to the ins and outs of working with your SFG and then move on to the more difficult crops when you've got a firm grasp of the system.

MEL'S TIP: A ROOF LIKE A WALL

In Square Foot Gardening, we grow a lot of plants vertically to save space and keep the plants healthy and producing. As you probably know, this involves building a vertical support with strong nylon netting. But did you know you can build the same kind of support horizontally? You see, some bushy plants, like peppers and eggplants, and many of the tall, long-stemmed flowers like dahlias are fine on their own until they get packed with heavy fruit or blossoms. Then the plant tends to fall over under the weight. Staking and tying these types of plants as is done in row gardens is just more work than most people will remember to do.

But there's a better, easier way to ensure that your peppers get the support they need; take the same idea we use vertically and turn it on its side! Use 3-foot metal stakes (steel pipe or fence post) at each corner of the box and then secure the nylon netting to each stake, making sure that it is stretched tightly from stake to stake. Early on, as your plants start to mature, they'll grow right through the netting. Then, when they grow all that great produce, the netting will support the plants without you having to do anything! Because the netting is soft yet strong and has large 6- × 6-inch openings, it's easy for the plants to just grow through it and there is nothing for you to do. Isn't that smart and easy?

Although the corner stakes used here are wood, you can use steel pipe if you want more secure supports, but always use the nylon netting—it's nearly indestructible!

Until recently, my onions were doing great. Now the tops are falling over. What am I doing wrong?

Not a darn thing! **It's completely natural** that the tops of your onions might become heavy and "lay down" as the onions mature. Once the tops go brown, it's time to harvest your onions, and you'll find them every bit as delicious as they would be if the tops had stood straight up.

I really only want to grow vegetables in my SFG. Is there any reason why I should include flowers?

Lots of reasons, actually. Flowers bloom, and insects love those pretty blooms every bit as much as we do (well, most of us). The blooms on a flowering plant will **attract many beneficial insects and birds to your SFG, and can repel others**. That's why gardeners regularly plant marigolds with their tomatoes. I think it's also important that your SFG be pretty. The better looking it is, the more you'll want to spend time there taking care of your garden. The more time you spend, the better your plants will do, and the more successful you'll be as a Square Foot Gardener. See where I'm going with that? Here's another reason for putting flowers in among your vegetables: You can eat them! Well, not all of them, but many flowers are edible and even tasty. If you want to see your kids' eyes grow big as saucers, sprinkle a few nasturtium and pansy blossoms over their next salad, or serve them chicken salad in a tulip—it tastes like apple! (Just be sure to clean out the inside of the tulip first, and wash it before serving.) If all that's not enough to convince you that flowers belong in your SFG vegetable garden, remember: You should always take time to stop and smell the flowers. You can't do that without flowers to smell!

❓ My beets are suffering even though I have them in the perfect spot and I think I did everything right. Any ideas?

❗ I'm going to tell you a little secret about beets (and broccoli too). They just love boron. **Boron is an essential micronutrient in soil**, and it can leach out of the soil when a lot of water moves through in a short period of time. So if you've experienced heavy rains off and on for awhile, your beets may be craving boron. Head to the local grocery store and pick up some Borax in laundry soap aisle. Then dissolve about ½ teaspoon in a quart of water, and water your beets. They should be back to their old selves in no time flat.

❓ Are there tricks to harvesting my SFG?

❗ First, expect to harvest a lot more than you would in a row garden. Because the SFG method leads to healthier plants with a lot less effort, they just produce a lot of vegetables and fruits. You may be used to all kinds of tools, but you can put them away, because harvesting an SFG requires just one: a good pair of scissors. I love a bargain, so I buy my scissors in August, during the back-to-school sales. Buy brightly colored children's scissors for about four bits apiece (well, that's what we called it when I was a boy, it's 50 cents these days). Colored scissors stand out more so you're less likely to misplace them, and they are so cheap that you can buy a pair for every box in your garden and leave them right by the box.

The actual harvesting couldn't be simpler. If you want a salad for dinner, just take your salad bowl right out to the garden and fill it by cutting the outer leaves of any lettuce, Swiss chard, parsley, beet leaves or mustard with those handy scissors. Round out your salad by pulling up a carrot or two and perhaps a radish. Wash your harvest by swishing it in a bucket of clean water you have just filled, later to

Continued

be used to water the garden, and you're ready to eat. If you harvest anything with a stem, like a tomato, pepper, bean, or pea, that's where the scissors come in again. Cut the fruit or vegetable from the stem rather than pull it off. If you pull it, you take a chance of damaging the main stem of the plant or even pulling it out of the ground, thus limiting the rest of your harvest.

Can't I just water all my SFG boxes at one time with an oscillating sprinkler?

I sure wish you wouldn't. That's a big waste of one of our most valuable resources, and it's just not necessary. It's easy to install drip irrigation lines in your SFG boxes, but **I much prefer hand watering**. Part of the benefit of an SFG is its smaller size. Watering by hand gives you a chance to check your plants for any problems, and you can do it at the same time you harvest fruits and vegetables. I always keep a bucket of water alongside my boxes, with a watering cup for each box. I just dip the cup in the water and give my plants a drink. For mature plants, just take one hand and pull back any bottom leaves so that you can water in the saucer-shaped depression right around where the stem goes into the soil. That way, you're putting the water almost directly into the roots. You also protect the plant from diseases that can occur when the leaves stay wet, and you'll save a tremendous amount of water. How much you may ask? An astounding 90 percent compared to a row garden. If you could reduce all of the costly items in your life down to only 10 percent, wouldn't that be worthwhile?

Now I know that this might seem a little tedious when you're watering several squares of smaller plants like carrots and radishes. So if you want to cheat a little, I suggest you try the "poor man's sprinkler." Put your fingers over the top of the watering cup and spread them out just a little so there are slight spaces between the fingers. Then shake out the water over the whole square. You give all the plants some water without washing away any soil. It's also a fun thing for the kids to do, and a great way to get them involved in the SFG experience!

❓ Won't large fruit like watermelon and cantaloupe fall off the plant if I grow them vertically?

❗ Not the way we do it. You see, nature is amazing and it has a way of compensating for growing conditions. We notice that the stems on all the heavy fruits and vegetables we grow vertically seem to be much thicker and stronger than others, holding the fruit up without any slings, or supplemental support. You just have to make sure the vertical frame and support are strong enough. That's why we make ours out of galvanized steel electrical conduit, and use nylon netting, which is unbreakable and has perfectly sized 6-inch-wide openings through which to train your plants.

Each week, you get to spend time with your vertical frames and just visit each plant. Tuck the ends in and out of the netting while you observe the plant's progress, the new leaves, or a new cluster of blossoms. You may spot a new sucker you need to prune on a tomato plant: if it has a few half-eaten leaves it could be the presence of the dreaded tomato hornworm. If you spot one, all hidden amongst the same color leaves, use your scissors to trim that half-eaten leaf and the worm and then dispose of them in the trash. No more damage there. Why not just pick him off the leaf? He has a way to spray you with a nasty smelling odor so I learned to just cut around him, and then no residual odor.

？ What is the logic behind all this vertical gardening? Isn't it easier to just let vining plants grow like they do in a row garden?

！ The logic behind vertical gardening, like the logic in everything about SFG, is to conserve space, effort, and resources while growing the same or better harvest than you would in a row garden. By growing vining plants—and other plants like tomatoes—on a strong sturdy support, we're able to grow more in a smaller area because we're going up, not out. The advantages don't stop there, though. With a little weaving of the plants through the strong nylon netting, you eliminate the need to tie plants up, getting rid of one more garden chore that always seemed to get away from you and then the plants broke off from the support as they grew. Of course some would say, that's why we let them crawl over the ground where they don't need support. But think of all the space you had to rototill, and fertilize. That's also why the row gardens were always way out back where you seldom visited, because the weeds took over by mid summer.

If you have trouble seeing that, think of a city that starts out all single story buildings and some guy comes along and says, "I'm going to invent a new way to construct buildings so we can have 10 stories in the same space as we used to have only one floor." You just reduced so many associated items, yet provided new and exciting things like a view for the residents.

But most importantly, **plants love to grow vertically**. Get them up off the ground and you protect them from rot and from lots of creepy crawlies such as slugs and snails. The plant gets more air circulation and grows stronger. Lastly, I have to say that a vertical wall of leafy growth, fruits, and vegetables is just a beautiful sight in the garden, and looks a lot more tidy and nicer than the same plants sprawling haphazardly all over the ground. It also makes them much easier to get close to without stepping on them and crushing a stem.

Does the nylon netting on my vertical support need to be very taut?

Yes it does. This ensures strong support and it just looks better.

Can I use a plastic trellis rather than the nylon netting for vertical support?

I'm certainly never opposed to people coming up with solutions that work better for them or improve on the SFG system. But I'm afraid **plastic trellis won't work** for the kind of vertical gardening we do in SFG. What you need is strength, and plastic just isn't going to cut it. Remember, in SFG, we not only grow tomatoes on our vertical supports, we grow watermelon, cantaloupe, and winter squash. Those are some heavy crops and you want to make sure they are well supported. I'd be leery of trusting a plastic—or wood—trellis, and I don't really know how you would adequately secure it.

Also, one of the things I really love about the nylon netting we use in SFG vertical gardening is the big openings—they allow you to easily weave plants right in and out of the netting so you don't need to waste a lot of time and effort tying your plants up (like you would on a trellis). I don't really like to say "no" too often, but I'd have to say the answer to a plastic trellis in your SFG is "no."

? Can I use PVC plumbing pipes or conduit for my vertical supports?

! You could in a pinch, but I wouldn't recommend it. You have to understand that when I was first developing SFG, I used both PVC and wood for the vertical supports, and they always broke and fell down. They look strong at first, but by the time the season is coming to a close, the plants are all the way to the top and the structure becomes very heavy with weight. A little wind can send the whole thing crashing to the ground. So that's when I said **no more wood, and no more PVC.** I decided to find a material that was strong, and I was thinking of steel fence posts. But then I found galvanized steel pipe in the electrical department of my local home center. This pipe is called "conduit," and it's what electricians use to run wiring through when they need to protect the wires. I use ½-inch conduit, which is very strong, and very inexpensive. As a bonus, it lasts practically forever and looks very nice in place. In my experience, you can't do better than that and why try?

? What vegetables should I grow on my vertical support?

All the vining vegetables should be grown on the vertical support. These include melons and cucumbers, as well as peas, pole beans, zucchini, and other summer and winter squashes. I also grow tomatoes and even watermelons on the vertical support. In fact, most of the fruits and vegetables that are allowed to sprawl out in row gardening are grown vertically in SFG. There are so many advantages, I don't know why anyone would allow their plants to crawl along the ground. Vertical gardening exposes the plants to more sunshine, and keeps them away from bugs and soil-borne diseases like rot. Besides, a wall of vegetables is quite attractive and looks very tidy. If you build your vertical support correctly, you'll be amazed at how strong it is and how many big and mature fruits and vegetables it can hold!

? Can I use my chain-link fence as a trellis?

The advantage of the large-opening nylon netting is that it eliminates all the tying-up of the vine crops. That makes gardening foolproof and easy, as well as increasing the harvest without having to study ground diseases and pests. Working with the chain-link alone, you will be faced with the need to tie up your plants.

That said, I think it would be a great idea to **use the nylon netting with the chain-link fence**. How about this: secure the netting to the fence at the top and stretch the netting 6 inches to 1 foot out from the fence all along the bottom using bamboo or electrical conduit for staking. Now you can weave the plants in and out of the netting, and the netting is supported by the strength of the chain-link fence.

I do have to emphasize, the fence should be on the north side of the SFG box if you going to use it as a vertical support so it doesn't shade the other plants in the box.

CHAPTER 4

WORKING WITH MEL'S MIX

If you love healthy, good food, then you know exactly how your plants feel. They are happiest when they have a consistent source of nutrients and water, and that source is always going to come from the soil in which they are rooted. Let me tell you, there is no better soil than the Mel's Mix we use in SFG. We call it the "perfect soil" because that's exactly what it is.

Mel's Mix is a basic formula but it provides everything your plants need to produce the biggest crop possible. In fact, time and time again we've seen gardeners grow tomatoes or peppers or squash in an SFG box full of Mel's Mix right next to a crop planted in the ground, and the Mel's Mix plants inevitably produce more—and bigger—vegetables and fruits. The benefits don't stop there, though.

Mel's Mix is also part of the "no work" notion of SFG. Row gardeners are forever preparing their soil for planting, using noisy, expensive, and gas-burning machines like a rototiller, or breaking their backs with shovels and picks, just to do the same thing the next year. That has always seemed a little crazy to me, and it's just a lot of effort that you don't need to expend. What's that old saying, "The definition of insanity is to keep doing the same thing but expect different results?" Mix up a batch of Mel's Mix, fill your boxes, and you're done. No more work every spring. Mel's Mix will last for at least 10 years. That's it. Buy a rocking chair instead of a rototiller.

The weeds are another reason why we use Mel's Mix in SFG. Weeding a garden is nobody's idea of fun, and is actually one of the worst parts of growing your own crops. Thank goodness, Mel's Mix eliminates the need for weeding. That's because your existing yard soil is chock-full of weed seeds. Plow it up and form rows for a garden, and you've just given those seeds the green light to grow like crazy.

But create a controlled medium like Mel's Mix, and weed seeds are banished. If and when the occasional weed seed ever does find its way into the box, it's a simple and easy thing to remove it because Mel's Mix is so loose. The weed and all of its root comes out—nothing to resprout like in row gardening, where you only chop off the top of the weed and then, since you fertilized all of the row garden soil, as soon as you turn on your garden sprinkler or hose, those weeds just sprout all over again. Does any of that make sense? So why are some people still doing row gardening?

"I am just amazed at how well things grow in Mel's Mix."

—Kathy from Ohio

As simple as Mel's Mix is, though, it's still relatively new and a lot of people (especially experts) have a hard time accepting and understanding anything new, so lots of questions do pop up about using it. What type of compost is best? What sort of vermiculite do we recommend? Where do you find vermiculite? What's the proper way to mix it so that you have three equal parts by volume rather than weight? The list goes on.

You'll find the answers in the pages that follow. I think reading through these discussions will give you more insight into the reasoning behind Mel's Mix, and will ensure that you, too, make the perfect soil for all your garden plants.

? Shouldn't I check the pH in my Mel's Mix from time to time?

 There's just **no need to do that**. I developed Mel's Mix as a perfectly balanced soil. Yes, peat moss is acidic, but the compost will effectively neutralize that acidity and maintain a nearly neutral pH for the soil. This makes Mel's Mix ideal for nearly any plant you would want to grow. It's one of my favorite simplifications of the method—no expensive testing required, no testing kits to buy, and no directions to read. (Despite the claims, they are not easy to use—believe me.) No extra learning or knowledge required. How easy is that?

> **SAFETY FIRST!**
> Blending Mel's Mix can be a dusty process. That's why I insist every Square Foot Gardener take precautions to avoid any health hazards associated with airborne dust.
>
> 1. Always wear a dust mask (the kind you wear when you're painting) when working with the three components of Mel's Mix.
> 2. Keep the little ones away. Children look at a big pile of dirt and think, "Wow, that would sure be fun to play in!" But they can crush the big pieces of vermiculite.
> 3. Use a hose with a very fine spray nozzle to mist the ingredients very lightly so you can keep the dust down as you work. NOTE: If you spray the ingredients instead of misting them, the mix will get soggy and perhaps even too heavy to work with.

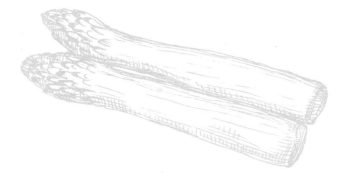

How full should my SFG boxes be before I start planting?

The soil should **come right up to the top** when you first fill the boxes, and it may settle slightly as the season goes on. That's normal, and remember, you will be adding a trowel of compost to each square foot as you replant each one. And don't worry. The box isn't going to overfill and spill out because everything gradually decomposes and settles a little bit. Remember I've thought ahead and tested every possible thing that could go wrong in order that you can have an enjoyable first time, or continued, gardening success.

? **A friend suggested that I might amend my soil, with lime if it's acidic, or sulfur if it's alkaline. How will I know if my SFG soil needs amending?**

! Here's an easy answer: **It doesn't.** I'm sure your friend has the best of intentions, and I'm also sure that he or she is a row gardener. Otherwise, that person would have realized there is no need to test the Mel's Mix in an SFG, nor is there any reason to amend it. Keep it simple people—using Mel's Mix couldn't be easier. Fill the box and let it be. Add a trowel of compost when you replant. And that's it. PS: All the ingredients in Mel's Mix are designed to end up in a neutral pH; and just about all plants will do well in it. So just forget all about pH, that's a relic of the row system where you use your existing soil. With SFG, everyone, no matter where they live in the country, starts off with a perfect soil. See how easy it can be?

? **How long does Mel's Mix last?**

! We have found it retains a good level of nutrients, and wonderful water and air retention properties **for about 10 years.** But of course remember: you're **adding new compost** constantly through the seasons, as you rotate from one crop and begin planting a new one. If you find through the years that the soil starts looking a little tired and not as good—not as loose and friable—you might start adding some Mel's Mix, or just vermiculite and peat moss each time you add a new crop. But you always regularly add a trowel of compost because that's where all the nutrients are.

❓ Can I amend or mix my Mel's Mix with some soil from my yard to save money?

❗ Absolutely not. My advice to anyone who wants to alter the Mel's Mix formula is always: **Don't mess with success!** I know the different elements of Mel's Mix might hit you in the wallet a little bit at the start, but since it lasts for 10 years with no additions except your one trowel of homemade compost every replanting, divide your first costs by 10 and that's it! Not so much after all, for a perfect soil and a perfect garden for 10 years. Look at it as an investment. Ten years equals a lot of vegetables on your table and a lot of savings from what you would have to buy in the supermarket, so you're going to have a return on that initial investment. In addition, yard soil is just chock full of those weed seeds we hate. Add yard soil to your Mel's Mix and you'll be introducing a whole lot of weeds to your SFG. I don't know about you, but I don't miss weeding at all, and the lack of weeds is one of my favorite things about SFG.

❓ Can I re-use vermiculite after sprouting seeds in it?

❗ Yes you can. All you need to do is **wash it** before you use it again.

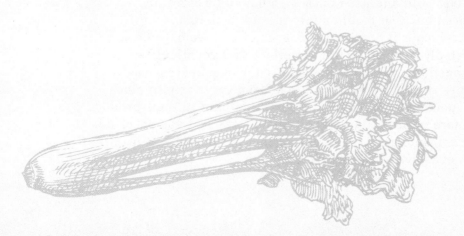

❓ Can I substitute expanded shale for vermiculite in my Mel's Mix?

❗ I'm going to have to advise that you don't. It's not that I mind people looking for alternatives, but **expanded shale is simply too heavy and gritty** for an SFG. It's going to make your Mel's Mix unpleasant to the touch and, more importantly, it won't retain moisture as well as vermiculite does.

❓ What about the risk of asbestos I've heard is associated with vermiculite?

❗ This issue comes up regularly, so it's worth dealing with head-on, once and for all. First, I'm a Square Foot Gardener and I don't want to endanger my own health; I'd never suggest other people do anything or use any material that I haven't already used. We at the SFG Foundation have taken a cold, hard, and long look at this issue. We've found that these concerns arise from an issue with a Montana mine, decades ago, in which some vermiculite was found to be contaminated with asbestos.

All our digging has led us to believe this was an isolated case. It was a serious incident and the mine was closed. But for some reason the incident keeps popping up as recent news. You know the old expression, on a slow news day, any old news is new news. Of course, any contaminated material that was sold and used back then has to be carefully removed but that would apply to, say, attic insulation, not new bags of horticultural vermiculite. We have been repeatedly assured by our suppliers that **vermiculite packaged for horticultural use today is asbestos-free.** Besides that, the government has been very vigilant since that incident—nobody wants a contaminant in their product. For more information on the topic, I'd suggest you check out the Environmental Protection Agency's comments at http://www.epa.gov/asbestos/vermfacts.pdf.

Where can I find the right vermiculite for my Mel's Mix?

Your best bet is to start at **local garden supply stores and nurseries**. Important!: Let your fingers do the walking. Give them a call and ask to speak to the manager, and then inquire if they carry the larger 4-cubic-foot bags of coarse vermiculite (it has to be coarse). Sometimes, even if they don't have the bags in stock, they can order them for you. If that doesn't pan out, check your Yellow Pages under "Greenhouse Supplies and Suppliers." If you find a good wholesaler, they may sell you the big bags directly from their factory—and at a better price than you can find elsewhere. I would also check with smaller nurseries and garden suppliers; sometimes they have vermiculite in the larger bags for their own use and will part with a bag if you ask nicely.

Farm supply stores are worth checking out, if there are any in your area. As a last resort, check with local swimming pool supply stores. Vermiculite is used in swimming pool filters. However, keep in mind that it must be "horticultural grade" vermiculite—no matter where you get it from. Whatever you do, don't drive from place to place—call first!

? What type of vermiculite should I buy for my Mel's Mix?

! Vermiculite is vermiculite. Regardless of the brand you buy, it's just mica—rock that's mined, ground up, and then cooked to over 2500°F, which pops the rock like popcorn. The one difference is that it comes in fine, medium, and coarse textures. **Always buy coarse vermiculite,** which holds more water, and the material will break down over the years into finer particles anyway. You can find vermiculite in smaller bags at large retailers and home centers, but I prefer the economy and easy use of the large 4-cubic-foot bags offered at garden centers and large nurseries.

? Are there any substitutes for using vermiculite in my Mel's Mix?

! I chose vermiculite as one of only three ingredients in my Mel's Mix specifically for it's fantastic water-retention properties, ease of air travel to the roots and perfect drainability when saturated. Nothing in soil holds and stores water quite like it! Take vermiculite out of the Mel's Mix and the soil won't drain properly. Although some people have tried substituting perlite, it floats to the top of the soil, looks unsightly, doesn't stay blended, doesn't hold water as well as vermiculite does and, to be honest, I have sneezing fits whenever I've worked with it! The fact is that vermiculite is available just about everywhere there is a garden supply store or nursery. Call ahead to find it. If they don't have it, ask them to get it in for you and the other millions of SFGers that are coming along. They will thank you for the tip.

? One of my SFG boxes is doing very poorly. The plants are not thriving, but there is no sign of pests or disease. Can a batch of Mel's Mix fail?

! Not likely. Is the soil in each and all of your boxes from the same source? Did you buy it all bagged? If so, take your receipt, a small handful of the soil, and the empty bag back to the store. If you mixed your own, the first place I would look would be the compost. Did you mix five different sources of compost? But the quickest way to figure out what's gone wrong in that box is to **take a soil sample to your local Cooperative Extension Service agent** for testing.

? Is all bagged manure composted?

! **Absolutely not.** Check the bag carefully and never buy manure that has not been composted. The excess nitrogen could wind up burning the plants in your SFG. It should not have a strong manure smell, but more of a subtle, maybe even pleasant, barnyard odor.

What size should I make my compost bin?

The minimum it should be is 2 × 2 × 2 feet, while the maximum is 4 × 4 × 4 feet. I find the ideal bin is right in between: 3 × 3 × 3 feet. The reason is, a compost pile that is too small won't heat properly, and one that is too large will keep air from the center so it will not heat up and be very slow to decompose.

I'm just starting to compost. I'd like to know how long it will take and how can I be sure the compost is ready to use?

Congratulations on joining the movement! On average, you can expect household and yard waste to decompose into compost in **4 to 8 weeks**. That assumes that you're turning and mixing the pile weekly, and checking to make sure that it's kept moist—not wet and not absolutely dry. Also, be sure to chop everything up before you add it, no big chunks. You can speed the timetable up a little bit by turning the pile more often. In any case, you know you have compost that's ready to add to your SFG boxes **when it's dark, fairly fine, and it clumps when you squeeze it**. It should smell woodsy but not rotten or moldy. You should not be able to identify any of the individual ingredients.

❓ What is the difference between potting soil and black dirt?

❗ Potting soil is made up of several different ingredients, all of which are usually organic. Just say no to any potting soil that contains commercial fertilizers of any kind. Black dirt, on the other hand, looks like rich, wonderful soil . . . until you discover that it's loaded with weed seeds. Three words: Don't buy it! Okay, if that didn't register, one word: NO!

If I have worms in my compost pile, does that mean it's really healthy?

I'm afraid not. Actually, if you have worms in your compost pile and they're the same as you find in the soil on your property, **something's wrong**, not with the worms but with your compost pile. Sounds like it isn't heating up and the worms are after all that good stuff you have in there. A compost pile is supposed to heat up to at least 140°F, making it an environment worms wouldn't be likely to inhabit. Certainly it's worth checking out the type of worm by taking a sample to a local nursery or your Cooperative Extension Service agent (put it in a baggie first). But the worms are a sign that the compost pile is either not being maintained properly, or that something is off in the composting process. You should turn your pile regularly, a minimum of once a week (something else that worms wouldn't like). Make sure that the pile is also being kept moist—not soaking wet and not dry—and that the ingredients you're adding are all organic and as finely chopped as possible.

Is it okay to add worm castings to the compost I use for my Mel's Mix?

Is it ever! **Worm castings are fantastic** in Mel's Mix and we encourage gardeners to add them whenever possible as one of the five sources of compost.

Can I add more Mel's Mix, instead of compost, when I rotate crops?

 I don't know why you would. That would be adding the most expensive parts of the soil mix, and it's just money you don't need to spend. The whole idea behind starting with Mel's Mix is that the compost in it will gradually decompose further and get used up. The plants will eventually consume all the nutrients so the compost has to be periodically replaced. The other two ingredients don't supply any nutrients—they're really just there to make the soil looser and more friable, and for water retention and drainability. So unless your soil has become compacted through the years, and noticeably less friable, there would be **no point in adding Mel's Mix**. Besides that, the directions are to add one trowel of compost so that that particular square foot gets recharged with enough nutrients for the next crop. If you add one trowel of Mel's Mix, you are adding just one-third of compost. Please everyone! Don't try to improve the system. I've worked for 30 years to make it simple and easy. Don't be like a music person and try to rearrange Beethoven's scores.

I'm going to blend the Mel's Mix for my SFG boxes, but I bought bulk (loose) compost. How do I make sure there are equal parts by volume?

This is a question I get fairly regularly, because compost bags may list the weight, but aren't labeled with cubic feet measurements. There's a simple way to deal with this: just **match shovelfuls or pails of each of the three ingredients** of Mel's Mix. I literally add a certain number of shovelfuls of peat moss and then the same number of compost and vermiculite. The pails or shovelfuls will be lighter or heavier, but that doesn't matter—you're matching the volume.

What are the best places to find the different types of compost I need for my Mel's Mix?

I'd start at your **local nurseries and garden centers**. They are most likely to have different types of compost. Remember, what you're looking for is at least five types of ingredients to use in the compost. This is probably going to take some label reading. For instance, many bags are a manure product. I was once asked if a gardener could count sheep, chicken, barnyard pigs, steer, and cow manure as the five ingredients, because that was five different animals. Noooo, that's five different manures and one of the five ingredients. I can't stress it enough: read that label. You might find a bag labeled rose food that could be a mixed-blend compost with worm castings. Wow! That's a great addition to your Mel's Mix.

Look specifically for bags listing multiple materials used in the compost (most are just one kind of organic material, such as steer manure). I don't know if I should tell you this but I never buy steer manure—for one reason. It's a *Far Side* cartoon I remember. Manure comes from all the steers that are lined up waiting to go in the slaughterhouse. Cow manure, or cattle manure, is from cattle grazing out in the hillside just coming in to be milked every day. Get the picture?

Also make sure that no chemicals or other additives, such as synthetic fertilizers, have been mixed into the compost. Shop around though. Large home centers usually stock up on things like compost at the beginning of the season, and you might find bags for a very good price. But even if you have to pay a bit more, keep in mind that with Mel's Mix, you're saving the cost of fertilizers.

Here's another possible source for you: many cities, towns, and counties have jumped on the environmental wagon and are now composting landscaping debris from the maintenance of parks and other public grounds. Often, the municipality will sell this compost for less than the bagged stuff, but you usually have to buy in bulk and haul it away (when gardening, it definitely pays to make friends with someone who owns a pickup truck!). Keep in mind though, that just about all of their ingredients are wood- and plant-based, so that is just one source.

CHAPTER 5

DEALING WITH PESTS, PETS AND OTHER PROBLEMS IN YOUR SFG

I designed Square Foot Gardening to be as easy as possible. I developed a planting layout and process that save resources, require less work, and guarantee more success than row gardening. I created a perfect soil in Mel's Mix to give plants everything they need season after season, year after year. And all that means that SFGs produce lush harvests of beautiful, delicious fruits and vegetables.

And that's the problem.

It's not just gardeners that love the bounty of an SFG. Insects, diseases, wildlife, and even your own pets are just as attracted to the harvest in your SFG. You can't trick Mother Nature; she knows a good thing when she sees it!

So it's inevitable that some Square Foot Gardeners are going to find themselves standing in front of their plants, looking at leaves full of holes or the empty space where ripe fruit had hung, scratching their heads and thinking, "What the heck?"

Figuring out just what's causing your problem is often as much of a challenge as solving the problem. Fortunately, SFGs are less likely to encounter pests, diseases, and other problems than row gardens are. It's yet another benefit of the small space and

"I would like to share my success. I have never gardened and am now a successful gardener due to my SFG! I am absolutely amazed . . . my gardening neighbors have praised my lush, deep-green plants. They are also surprised at the success I've had with certain vegetables they've struggled with. I tend to my garden while still in my suit after work without getting dirty. This experience has been absolutely thrilling!"

—Lani in Arizona

controlled environment of an SFG. Just the same, this chapter is written to answer real questions about pests and help you out with the rare problem that might crop up. We've addressed all the different types of problems gardeners encounter, from insect pests big and small, diseases of all kinds, dealing with wildlife and domestic animals, and protecting against day-to-day damage from the errant softball or game of tag.

But no matter what the solution, the first goal should always be to not make the problem worse. You're not doing your garden a favor if, in getting rid of a troublesome pest you kill beneficial insects like bees at the same time. You'll also only add to your frustration if you jump in with a solution before you even are certain what the problem is. I see that a lot with people asking questions about plant damage or signs of insect infestation in online forums. A thousand guesses and nobody is certain what it really is. Sometimes it really pays to take the time and effort to consult a professional like the local Cooperative Extension Service agent or nursery professional. Remember, you want to keep your garden healthy no matter what treatment you use to deal with a problem.

So look through the chapter and pick out the solutions for the problems you're dealing with, and keep the book nearby for any others that may pop up during the season.

？ How do I save my squash plants from these disgusting squash bugs?

！ Squash bugs can proliferate quickly and they are tough to eradicate, so it's important to take action at the first sight of one. The larvae and young bugs are much easier to kill than the mature individuals. They are slow moving and easy to catch, so handpicking can be an effective control method. Drop mature bugs into a jar of warm soapy water, and knock or brush eggs from the undersides of leaves into the same jar. You can destroy these bugs and the eggs by just squishing them, but I wouldn't recommend this. They are relatives of the stinkbug and you'll find out just how closely related they are when you squish them. You'll think they're second cousins! Some gardeners have had success with Neem oil, but this usually isn't effective against adult squash bugs. I would suggest hitting them early and often with **physical removal**, and making sure there is no yard debris about that could shelter the bugs. Other than that, healthy plants are your best defense against the damage these bugs can cause.

Notice above the importance of **catching a problem like this early,** when there's just eggs or small bugs. Much easier to control. Remember how I tell people that with a big single row garden way out back you only visit it a couple times a week and the bugs can get a good foothold before you even notice them. Then it's almost too late. With your Square Foot Garden, you tend it regularly, and with hand watering, you nurture your plants; you'll see the bugs right away. You'll see the first sign of something wrong, and then it's much easier to take care of. It's just like nurturing your children. If you only see them twice a week, you don't notice they have the sniffles. Then they come down with a cold, which turns into a serious illness. Then it's too late to correct. Catch it when they still have a runny nose—and tend your gardens the same way. That's why I like to encourage people to treat their plants like their children.

What should I do about small spots of fungus on my plants?

SFGs don't usually have many problems with fungus because of the careful way we water and because in keeping plants up off your yard soil you protect them from fungi. Still, on the odd chance your plants are affected, here's a homespun solution: **water the plant once a week with a solution of one Bayer's children aspirin dissolved in a cup of water**. Just make sure you water only the affected plant; this solution should not be used on healthy plants.

I've just seen a cockroach around my SFG box. How do I nip this problem in the bud?

Cockroaches are pretty durable pests and they aren't confined to the inside of the house, but there are several ways to fight them inside or out. For a totally natural solution, you might try **chopping up cucumber skins and bay leaves and spreading the mixture all around** where you've seen the roaches. Another organic solution is to make a tea with catnip in hot water, and strain out the leaves. Spray the infested area with the tea, reapplying every couple of days. As a final step, turn to the tried-and-true cockroach killer: Mix two cups of borax (you'll find it in the detergent aisle at your local supermarket), ½ cup sugar, ½ cup of chopped onion, 2 tablespoons cornstarch, and 2 tablespoons water. Mix the ingredients well and roll the moist mixture into small balls, about the size of a marble. Place two or three in an unsealed sandwich bag in a place where kids and pets cannot get them, but the roaches will. Roaches love these toxic treats and are quickly eliminated.

COMMON SFG PESTS AND SOLUTIONS

Into every garden some pests must come. The pests you're likely to deal with depends on where you live, local climate, the plants you grow, and other variables. The first step in fighting any pests that threaten your SFG is to correctly identify them. The best way to do that is to take a sample of the critter or damage it does (in a resealable plastic bag) to your local Cooperative Extension Service agent or reputable nursery professional. Once you know what you're dealing with, the general process always involves starting with the mildest solution and working your way up to more powerful treatments as needed.

WILDLIFE AND LARGE PESTS

Dogs: Fence out the neighbor's pet, restrain yours with a leash; prevent damage from both with wire cage

Cats: Wire cage preferred; plant rue; sprinkle repellent garlic powder mix (page 136)

Woodchucks: Epsom salt around soil and plants; predator urine around perimeter of yard and boxes

Deer: Wire cage; pepper spray

Raccoons: Wire cage; moth flake barrier; pepper spray

Large Birds/Blue Jays, Crows: Netting; false predators; predator noises

RODENTS AND VERMIN

Squirrels: Cheesecloth or screen netting over plants

Chipmunks: Wire cage; pepper spray

Rats: Wire cage; live or kill traps; outdoor cats

Mice & Voles: Live or kill traps; predator urine; outdoor cats

Gophers: High-quality weed barrier (landscaping fabric); chicken wire under box; solid bottom on box; live gopher trap (sonic stakes and other sonic devices rarely work long term)

INSECTS

Cabbage Moth/Cabbage Worm: Plant rosemary; protective netting early season; Bt spray (early season); handpicking worms; dust cabbage plant leaves with flour

Tomato Hornworm: Plant marigolds; Btk spray in early season; introduce predator wasps

Mosquitoes: Plant lemongrass; remove stagnant water or cover standing water with a few drops of vegetable oil; DEET spray on clothing and exposed skin; citronella candles

Wasps (non-beneficial): Sugar trap (page 122); remove ripe fruit

Gnats: Vodka spray (page 120); sprinkle diatomaceous earth on top of soil near infestation

Japanese Beetle: Plant geraniums; handpick; neem oil in early season; insecticidal soap spray; trap (page 130)

Leafhopper: Protective netting early in the season; wash from leaves with jet of water; insecticidal soap; sticky traps; neem oil, beneficial insects such as parasitic wasps

Flea Beetle: Plant catnip and garlic; garlic spray; sticky traps and handpicking; dust with diatomaceous earth; beneficial nematodes in spring; organic pyrethrin spray as last resort

Thrips: Wash off leaves; insecticidal soap; neem oil

Aphids: Insecticidal soap; citrus spray; garlic spray; or Neem oil; dust with diatomaceous earth; beneficial insects such as parasite wasp or lady beetle

Ants: Citrus sprays (directly on the ants, on anthills, and around boxes and plants); cornmeal sprinkled around anthills; carefully pour boiling water down nest

Spider Mites: Buttermilk spray (page 123); salt spray (page 128) or garlic spray (page 129); predatory mites for heavy infestations

Squash Bugs: Plant catnip; handpick and drown in soapy water; Neem oil when immature; organic pesticide such as rotenone for excessive infestations

SAFETY FIRST!

I'm really opposed to broad-spectrum insecticides, pesticides and fungicides. Pests and diseases are far less of a problem in an SFG than they might be in a row or other type of garden, so the strong solutions are rarely called for. These chemicals are usually very effective on a particular pest, but their effectiveness does not stop there. More often than not, they will also kill beneficial insects and organisms. The active components of these products can settle into the soil and stay there for a good long time. Personally, I don't want strong chemicals around plants I'm going to eat. This includes sprays and powders made from natural sources such as chrysanthemums and geraniums. These too, can be toxic. Always read labels carefully and completely, and start fighting any garden intruder with the mildest solution first.

The gnats in my SFG have become a real bother. Is there a way to deal with these annoying insects?

I know how irritating gnats can be, especially when you're hot and sweaty—they seem to love to crowd you. Here's what you do: Make a spray by **mixing 1 part vodka with 3 parts water**. No, don't drink it, spray the area infested by the gnats. By the way, you can check whether you've gotten rid of the gnats by cutting a potato in half and leaving it in the area. If, after a week, the potato is still clean, your gnat problem is solved.

❓ Any ideas for getting rid of pesky fruit flies?

❗ No problem. Spray your harvest with a half-and-half mix of **rubbing alcohol and water** in a spray bottle. The fruit flies will immediately disperse, and the alcohol will evaporate soon after.

❓ What can I do about my tomato blossom end rot?

❗ First, take heart. You're not alone. Blossom end rot—a condition in which the fruit of the plant has ugly brown deformed bottoms—is a fairly common disorder (just be glad it's not you). It's caused by a lack of calcium in the plant and is easily remedied with, of all things, Epsom salt. Yes, that stuff you use for soaking your bad back in the bath! If you know your tomato plants are susceptible to blossom end rot, **dig a cup of Epsom salt into the Mel's Mix** of the square in which you'll grow the plants, at the start of the season. If you're dealing with a case of rot in progress, remove the affected fruit and water the plant or plants with **½ cup of Epsom salt dissolved in a gallon of water**. By the way, you can use Epsom salt to improve the health of all your plants; it promotes robust root growth and resistance to disease. It never hurts to add ½ cup to your sun-warmed water bucket.

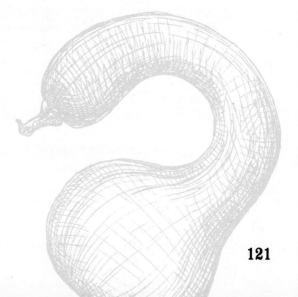

What should I do about millipedes and centipedes? They are so creepy.

Creepy? Perhaps. Bad for the garden? No. So the answer is, **"Nothing."** As ugly as they may be, centipedes are insect hunters—including many insects you don't want in your garden. They stun the insect with venom, but their venom claws aren't strong enough to pierce human skin, even if they wanted to. Millipedes are even less bother to humans. They look like worms with many legs, but feed on rotting organic matter such as wood, and rarely go after seedlings or leaves.

How can I convince the wasps in my yard that they should go somewhere else?

I think the first question is really, "Do you really want them out of your yard." I know that larger aggressive wasps, like the mud wasps that build their homes on a structure, and burrowing wasps, can be a threat in your yard, especially for anyone who is allergic. But keep in mind that smaller parasitic wasps can be hugely useful in controlling destructive insects such as aphids. If you do decide you need the wasps out of your yard and life, **mix 1 cup sugar with 1½ cups water in a wide-mouth jar**. Wasps will be attracted to the sugar, but will drown in the water. Be careful though: place the jar (or jars if you have a large yard) far away from the garden—perhaps along the side of garage or in a shed. You don't want to attract additional wasps into the garden. For the same reason, make sure you pick or remove all fruit from your garden as soon as it ripens. Wasps feed on nectar and will be drawn to a garden full of ripening or rotting fruit.

Can you suggest a treatment for spider mites?

I can suggest more than one. First, though, you should be sure you have spider mites. It's rare that SFGs are bothered by pests, so you need to identify them. These are tiny insects that will look like dots on your leaves (usually the underside) and look just like spiders under a magnifying glass. A few mites won't cause much of a problem, but a colony can sap a plant by sucking the leaves dry. The problem becomes evident as leaves yellow and die, and you may notice broad, finely woven webs. A couple simple sprays should take care of any spider mite population. The first is **a well-blended mix of ½ cup flour, 2½ gallons water, and ½ cup of buttermilk.** Sound's delicious, but spider mites don't think so. You can also go more basic with a spray of 1 to 1 rubbing alcohol to water. Either way, spray the plant thoroughly, including the undersides of leaves. You may need to reapply the spray two or three times before you entirely rid the garden of spider mites. For big infestations, you can turn to a common organic control of predatory mites. Order these mites online and release them near the affected plants, and they'll make short work of your spider mite population without bothering your plants.

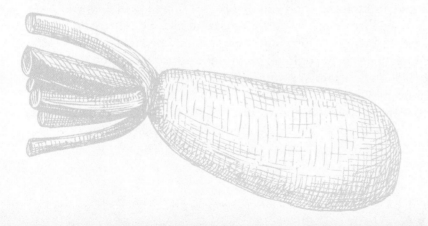

? I think the mosquitoes in my garden are going to drive me crazy. Any advice?

! If mosquitoes are a problem in your area, you'll want to **get rid of any other breeding grounds—standing water in coffee cans, tires, puddles,** or anywhere else. Don't worry about your bucket of sun-warmed water. Keep a watch out for eggs and pupa (they wiggle on the surface) and discourage mosquitoes of any age with a squirt or two of vegetable oil. In any case, you're usually using the water and refilling your bucket regularly, and mosquitoes need time to lay their eggs, hatch, and turn into a flying adult. (By the way, did you know that only the female bites and consumes blood? No letters ladies, I'm only reporting the facts, not the reasons.)

You can also **use a citrus spray or DEET spray** on your skin (or better yet, on your clothing) when working in the garden at any time that mosquitoes are active (usually around dusk or dawn). Citronella candles or torches filled with citronella oil are both effective against mosquitoes. Station one at each SFG box in your yard. I'd also recommend that you wear **light-colored clothing**—long-sleeve shirts and long pants—when working in the garden; mosquitoes like to stay hidden and will avoid light-colored surfaces.

> **⚠ SAFETY FIRST!**
> There are lots of things you can do to protect your SFG from your pets, but did you know that you might need to protect your pets from your SFG? Depending on what you grow, your garden can be a dangerous place for your best friends and housemates. You might be surprised to learn that a number of common vegetables, herbs, and flowers can be toxic and even deadly for house pets. Dogs can be poisoned by dock and geraniums, and cats should avoid jade, tulips, and yarrow. Both dogs and cats can be sickened by ingesting parts of garlic, onions, tomato plants, chives, aloe, begonia, daffodils, lantana, rhubarb, St. John's wort, and more. For a comprehensive list, go to the ASPCA's website at www.aspca.org/Pet-care/poison-control/Plants. Better yet, just take steps to keep pets out of your SFG and everyone will be happy!

? Our collard greens, broccoli, cauliflower, and cabbage have been hit hard by little green caterpillars (white moths too) that I think are cabbage worms. How do we get rid of them?

! Now I'll say this a lot—you need to be sure of the pest. It's so rare that SFGs are troubled by pests that Square Foot Gardeners usually are not used to identifying them. The best way to know what you are dealing with is to bring one of them to a nursery professional or County Cooperative Extension Service agent. Once you have a clear identity, you can be sure you're using the right treatment. In your case, it does sound exactly like the common cabbage worm that we see all over the country. The caterpillars are small and green, the butterflies are dirty white with dark gray or black spots on the wings.

Keep in mind that one of the wonderful things about an SFG is how compact it is; **handpicking the caterpillars** can be an effective control method. Some people have mentioned home remedies that you might try, including **dusting the plant with flour**—the caterpillar eats the flour and it combines with the moisture in the worm to puff up and kill the insect. When spraying or dusting for cabbage worms— and other worms for that matter—always make sure you get the undersides of the leaves. If the caterpillars continue to be a problem, **you can spray with Bt** (*Bacillus thuringiensis*), an organic spray that kills the caterpillar as it feeds. Follow the directions on the label to the letter. Prevent these persistent pests next year by **covering the plants with floating row covers**, netting that prevents the moth from laying her eggs in the first place. She'll now have to go next door to your neighbor's single row garden where there are plenty of cabbages all in a row for her to land on.

? How can I get rid of ants?

! Not all ants are created equal, but most will respond to a very simple, organic treatment. Boil the peels of several oranges in a quart of water, let cool, and then strain the liquid into a spray bottle. Find the anthill and liberally spray the area, as well as all around your SFG box. The citrus oil can burn the ants' bodies and the ants aren't fond of orange scent, so they'll head for greener pastures. If you don't want to make your own, you'll find **citrus-based insect sprays** in the garden aisles at local home centers and at nurseries. Be careful when spraying aggressive ant species that bite or sting, such as fire ants or army ants. Spraying directly on the ants may anger them and make them attack. If you have a problem with aggressive ants in your yard, spray around your plants and along the foundation of your home.

Here's another remedy that should work for just about any ants: **sprinkle cornmeal liberally around an anthill**. The ants eat the dry stuff and it then becomes moist and swells and . . . well . . . no more ants. You can also pour boiling water down their nests.

SAFETY FIRST!
Many home remedies for getting rid of garden pests have been handed down by generation after generation. Some were actually suggested as a spoof but were successful enough to get passed on. Others might work most of the time, but many could actually cause damage if used in excess or in too strong a dose. A friend who is a County Extension agent in Florida recommends caution when using home remedies. Here's what he has to say: "I am always cautious with 'home remedies' because of all the additives that are in new formulations of soaps, that were not there when our grandparents first used them."

I think he is right that you need to be cautious and question what you read and use. For example, I have read if you don't want to pick up slimy slugs on your night slug patrol, just use a salt shaker to shake it on them like you would on your food. But that could be too much and you would harm your plants and soil. You could always use a glove or my suggestion—an old-fashioned long hatpin or ice pick to place them in a cup of salt water. Don't spill any on your plants. In summary, exercise common sense, caution, and moderation.

MEL'S TIP: FLOWER POWER!

Some flowers are well-known to repel insects. Planting these flowers can help keep your other plants—especially fruits and vegetables—pest free. Although it's not an exact science, planting these flowers may help you in your fight to keep your other plants safe.

- Marigolds are considered natural companions for tomatoes because the scent of the marigold is repulsive to many kinds of beetles and tomato hornworm.

- Lemongrass helps repel mosquitoes from the garden.

- Nasturtiums can dissuade white flies and woolly aphids from calling your SFG home.

- Garlic is a naturally great pest repellent, sending away a variety of insects, including flea beetles, Japanese beetles, borers, aphids, spider mites, and more. There are many different types of garlic that you can plant, but all are associated with insect-repellant properties.

- Rue is a nasty flower to flies and Japanese beetles, and it will also keep dogs and cats away from other plants.

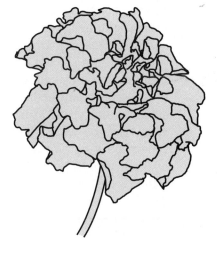

- Lavender is said to keep mice away, and is a deterrent to many different bugs, including moths, whiteflies, and even bed bugs. Some gardeners even plant it as an insect-repellant fence around the property.

- Some types of geraniums have a negative effect on Japanese beetles and cabbage worms.

- Catnip is considered effective in repelling flea beetles, Japanese beetles, and squash bugs, among other insects. Just keep in mind that it's also a powerful attraction to neighborhood cats.

- Rosemary can work against cabbage moths and carrot flies, as well as some other insects.

ORGANIC PESTICIDE SPRAYS

There are a number of organic alternatives to more powerful and harmful chemical pesticides on the market. Remember to always start with the weakest, mildest solution and work up from there. Keep in mind that even though these are organic, that doesn't mean they are entirely harmless. In some cases, organic sprays may eliminate beneficial insects such as bees or lady beetles along with the insect you're targeting. Take care when spraying to avoid direct spray on bees, lacewings, earthworms, and other insects you don't want to hurt. Regardless of the spray you use, don't spray the leaves of a plant during a hot sunny day because you may cause leaf burn. Spray early in the morning or in the early evening. Keep all these sprays away from children, clearly labeled and stored in a cool, dry area. Wash your hands after working with sprays, and avoid any contact with your eyes. When spraying plants, always make sure to spray the undersides of the leaves as well. Sprays must be reapplied regularly to be effective, especially right after rainfall.

SOAP SPRAY: Although you can buy insecticidal soap spray over the counter at most nurseries, it's just as easy (and less expensive) to mix your own. Add 3 tablespoons of organic, non-detergent dishwashing soap (Ivory is a good choice for this) to 1 gallon (4 quarts) of water. Then spray the affected plants—insects get stuck, coated and smother. Soap spray is extremely effective on aphid infestations.

SALT SPRAY: Salt spray desiccates insects, killing them by drying them out. Use Epsom salt, which is not only benign to plants, it can aid in soil and plant health. Mix ½ cup of Epsom salt in one gallon of warm water. Salt spray works well on cabbage worms and spider mites.

CITRUS SPRAY: Add a nice aroma to your SFG while you fight off insect infestations with this simple spray that you cook up in your kitchen. Peel 1 or more lemons or oranges and boil the rinds in a quart of water. Let cool and leave overnight. Then strain the water and add a few drops of biodegradable organic dishwashing soap. Spray affected plants thoroughly. The spray is most powerful against soft-bodied insects, like aphids, because it burns their bodies. The scent will repel other insects.

GARLIC SPRAY: Garlic is one of the most universally effective pest treatments because insects just hate it. Chop up a large head of garlic and a large onion, and soak them with 1 tablespoon cayenne pepper in about 1 quart warm water. Strain and fill a spray bottle with the water mixed with a few drops of organic, biodegradable dishwashing liquid. Spray your plants liberally. You'll need to spray again every couple of days and for a week after all insects disappear. This spray can be used to kill or repel slugs, cutworms, whiteflies, aphids, and many other insects.

PEPPER SPRAY: Boil 2 tablespoons cayenne pepper in a quart of water for about 10 minutes. Let the mix cool, and then fill a spray bottle. This is a simple and easy way to coat your plants with a non-toxic spray that repels many insects, but also sends deer, raccoons, and other wildlife packing.

NEEM OIL: Neem oil is the next line of defense beyond homemade sprays. Mix 1 tablespoon in 2 quarts water and spray the entire plant. It is extremely effective in fighting leaf-eating insects, including whitefly, aphids, Japanese beetles, moth larvae, and spider mites. Neem oil is also used as fungicide to fight attacks of rust, blackspot, mildew, leaf spot, scab, anthracnose, blight, and botrytis.

DIATOMACEOUS EARTH: This is not a spray, but a dust applied with a special applicator. But like the sprays listed, diatomaceous earth is an all-natural, non-toxic solution to many insect pests. It is made from shell fossils ground up into a powder. It has a sharp, crystalline structure that slices the protective coatings or shells of insects as they pass over or through the dust, or shreds their digestive system when consumed. The insects quickly dry out and die. DE is a powerful tool for use on a wide range of insects, including slugs, aphids, flea beetles, thrips, borers, and more. It won't harm plants, but it should not be inhaled, and you should use both a dust mask and eye protection when applying DE.

❓ I just found Japanese beetles on my eggplant plants. How can I head off any more damage?

❗ We find that SFG plants are rarely attacked by Japanese beetles, but if you've ever grown roses, you'll be very familiar with this pest. Many people are surprised to discover that Japanese beetles love strawberries, beans, rhubarb, and your prized eggplants, as well other veggies. There are a number of ways to control them, but you have to be smart about how you do it.

Too many people, in my opinion, head right out to the garden center and buy one of the over-the-counter solutions. Pheromone traps draw beetles into a sticky trap using powerful hormones, but the hormones usually draw as many new beetles to your yard as you catch. I'd suggest you start by simply **handpicking the beetles**. They are slow and easy to pluck. If this doesn't do the trick, use this recipe for a homemade trap that a Square Foot Gardener gave me: **Mix 1 cup warm water, 1 cup sugar, 1 well mashed ripe banana, and 1 package yeast in a plastic gallon milk jug.** Place the jug far away from your SFG boxes with the top off, either on the ground or hung from a tree. The rotting odor will attract the beetles, who climb into the jug but can't get out. Be prepared that, just as with a pheromone trap, you may be drawing all the beetles from your neighbors' yards.

Both **Neem oil and insecticidal soap** can be effective against Japanese beetles, but must be sprayed directly on the beetles to kill them. Lastly, if you are willing to go with a messy-looking solution, sprinkle self-rising flour over whatever plant the Japanese beetles are attacking, and the beetles will head right over the fence to your neighbor's house!

? What's the best way to deal with aphids on tomato plants?

! Oh boy, those aphids. Aphids are some of the most common garden pests, and they can be quite bothersome. They'll attack the young succulent growth on many of your vegetable plants and, if you have them on your tomatoes, chances are that you might find them on your cabbage or bell peppers tomorrow. Luckily, aphids are some of the easiest insect pests to control, especially within the confines of a SFG. **Simply squashing aphids on the leaf** can send out a chemical signal that causes nearby aphids to drop and flee. You can also remove them from plants with **blast of water from the hose**—just make sure you don't damage your plants.

Start with a simple spray of **insecticidal soap**. You can find bottles of this at nurseries, home centers, and many general retailers. Or you could make your own and save a little money. Add a teaspoon of all-natural non-detergent dishwashing soap to a quart of water, and mix in a splash of canola oil, then pour the mixture in a spray bottle and spray your plant leaves top to bottom. The really natural way to deal with the problem is to **introduce natural predators,** or what are known as beneficial insects. These include lady beetles (what most people call ladybugs) and lacewings. You can find them at many larger nurseries.

Garlic sprays are also incredibly effective against aphids. Combine three cloves of chopped-up garlic, in 16 ounces of water, with a teaspoon of mineral oil. Let the mixture sit for two days, strain the fluid into a large measuring cup, add a couple squirts of Ivory dish soap, and fill a spray bottle. Then spray right on the aphids.

Mix yourself up a spray bottle's worth of this home remedy and say goodbye to aphids on your tomatoes.

131

How should I deal with leaf miners on my zucchini plants?

That depends on how much damage they're doing. First, you need to understand that leaf miners aren't one pest, they're many. They are basically the larvae of different butterflies, moths, and flies. They can, in some cases, do serious damage because if they destroy enough leaves the plant won't be able to perform the necessary photosynthesis it needs to grow. In many instances, just trimming off the damaged parts of leaves and throwing them away can limit the harm leaf miners will do. If you do need to control leaf miners on your SFG plants, start with a simple, organic solution like Neem oil. The oil is sprayed on the leaves weekly until the leaf miners are eradicated. Another organic treatment is called spinosads, which is also sprayed onto the leaves. However, spinosads can be dangerous to beneficial bees, so it's usually only used in serious cases where you're in danger of losing several plants to leaf miner damage. Both Neem oil and spinosads should be used strictly according to the label directions.

MEL'S TIP: A BEERY GOOD SOLUTION TO SLUGS AND SNAILS

Slugs and snails just love beer, and luckily they aren't committed to any particular brand! Simply fill a shallow saucer with any leftover beer and place the saucer wherever you've seen evidence of slugs or snails—trails or eaten leaves. The beer can be left there for several days and you should remove any drowned slugs or snails you find. Of course, if you're not a beer drinker, but you're willing to do a little night hunting, bring your best flashlight along with a sharp awl or ice pick and a paper cup full of salty water and go on slug patrol. Do it every night at the same time to thoroughly eradicate slugs and snails from the garden. Can you guess how you do it? Get down close to your plants with your flashlight and any time you see one of the devils, impale them with your ice pick and drop them into the salty water.

What can I do about the flea beetles that are attacking my peppers and other plants?

There's no need to let these insects get the better of you. I know they cause a lot of damage to a lot of different types of vegetables, and it looks terrible—almost like someone blasted the leaves with a shotgun. But your plants can recuperate if you get rid of the little demons. There's a lot of talk about breaking up plantings with flowers and other plants that the flea beetle may not care for, but I don't think that's a comprehensive solution, especially when you've already got an infestation on your hands.

Some people also use sticky traps placed around the affected plants, and simple hand picking. But I think that's a lot of work and probably isn't going to rid your garden of the entire population of beetles. Your best bet is going to be **dusting the plants and soil with diatomaceous earth**. This organic product is made from ground-up shell fossils and has a crystalline structure that slices the beetles' protective shells, leaving them open to drying out and dying. You'll find diatomaceous earth at nurseries and large garden centers, along with applicators for spraying the earth onto the plants. Be sure and use a dust mask and eye protection when working with this material—you don't want it in your lungs or eyes.

As a last resort—if you're just overrun by flea beetles, you can use an organic pesticide such as pyrethrin spray, which is made from chrysanthemums. The only problem is that you'll be poisoning beneficial insects as well. You can make sure you don't have the same problem next year, **by spraying your yard soil with beneficial nematodes** at the start of the season, which will kill any beetle larvae before they have a chance to mature. You can also lay down thick plastic sheets over your Mel's Mix, which may stop the larvae from hatching.

How do I prevent termites from destroying my SFG box and getting into my Mel's Mix?

Have I got a solution for you! Not only is it going to help you protect your SFG boxes from termites, you can use this trick to outwit snails, slugs, ants, and other creepy crawlies that can't swim. The trick is to **elevate the box and block access to the insects**. You see, termites live in the ground. They come up into wet and weakened wood structures to feed. So we're going to raise your box up by putting a plywood bottom on it just as you would if you were making a tabletop SFG (it's as easy as can be—you just screw a 4 × 4 section of plywood to the undersides of all the box sides, don't forget to drill ¼-inch drainage holes under each square foot and in each box corner). Then we're going to sit the box up on simple legs made of two concrete blocks per leg (you can find square concrete blocks at just about any home center, and you can substitute bricks if you can't find the blocks). Stack the blocks for each leg, but separate them with a two-flange metal collar—you can find these at large home centers or hardware stores.

This may look a little funny, but it works like a dream. The crawling insects try to get up those legs to the tasty wood in your box, but they just can't get around the metal collar that sticks out between the two blocks. It's like a mountain climber who has to climb out over a ledge sticking out from the side of the mountain, and the insects just can't do it!

If you want to make your box even more secure, position shallow trays underneath each block leg and fill them with water. Then, the insects will not only face a big climb, they'll also need to swim to get to the legs. Just be sure to squirt a couple drops of liquid dishwashing soap or vegetable oil in the trays; that will stop any mosquitoes from making a home in the water.

Another way to easily make insect-preventing legs is to screw 6-inch-long carriage screws into the bottom of your box and sit those in Cool Whip containers of water. You may have to eat a lot of Cool Whip and fresh strawberries, so start saving up those or similar containers.

❓ How can I make sure that cutworms won't be a problem for the tomatoes in my SFG?

❗ One of the advantages of SFG is that there is no concentration of any one type of plant, like in a long row of just one thing. We spread out the same plants and make it difficult for the pests to just go from one plant to another of their favorite dishes, which is why they are there in the first place. In a recent survey of pests, they have nicknamed SFG "Slim Pickings" because you have to walk too far to find your next course. That's because of what we call "selective separation." Plant one cabbage plant over there, one over here and another one in another SFG box and you make it awfully difficult for the insects to move from one meal to the next. The insects are more likely to migrate to a row garden, where the cabbages are laid out like a landing strip.

That is one of the key reasons we **plant squares in each box with different species**—it's the perfect way to stop diseases and pests from spreading. The small, contained size of an SFG box means that you're more likely to notice invaders early on, when you can take action right away before the problem gets out of hand. Handpicking most small crawlers and leaf eaters will be an effective way to rid your plants of troublemakers. If the problem is a little more severe, turn to organic sprays or treatments—but avoid toxic chemical pesticides. The residue will settle into your Mel's Mix and affect all your other plants.

Do I have to worry about gophers, moles, or voles in my SFG box?

Tunneling pests can be a real headache for any gardener, but are not a common concern for Square Foot Gardeners. You see, you're already protecting your plants with the weed barrier that goes underneath your Mel's Mix. That will block most of these critters (gophers and voles eat the plants; moles are insect-eaters that cause plant root damage with their tunneling). If tunnelers are big problem in your neck of the woods, you can take extra precautions to protect all your delicious plants. As you can imagine, voles and gophers prefer to dig through nice, soft dirt. They really don't like their paws to come in contact with sharp metal edges. That's why the best deterrent is a **wire product called hardware cloth**, available at your local hardware or home building store. It comes in a roll; buy by the foot only what you need. Place it under your box to block these vermin.

Voles tend to be a little bolder and tunnel near the surface. You can keep them out of your box by limiting the amount of soft, loose mulch you use (they just love to move under cover of a layer of straw) and by working in your box often, because they don't like to encounter humans. If the tunnelers in your yard get out of hand, the final solution is to use a trap—you can find kill-type "scissors" traps that are set right over a tunnel, or humane live traps that are set into a tunnel and removed when you capture an animal (you'll need to relocate the tunneler at least several miles from your home).

MEL'S TIP: SAYING NO TO SQUIRRELS

Squirrels are thieves that love nothing better than to take the crops you've worked hard to grow, eat a bit, and leave the rest lying on the ground. Or they love to bury their harvest of acorns in spots where the digging is easy. Guess where? Repel these varmints by sprinkling a dry mixture of 1/3 cup flour, 2 tablespoons cayenne pepper, and 2 tablespoons of garlic powder, all around your SFG box. Keep in mind that you'll have to sprinkle the mixture again after any rainfall. Or, the most positive and foolproof way to protect your SFG is to build one of the good-looking wire cages described on page 51.

How do I keep the neighborhood cats from using my SFG box as a litter box?

Cats just love Mel's Mix. They are actually convinced that I designed the formula just for them, to be used as their own personal litter box. But no Square Foot Gardener wants to head out to their garden to pick some delicious vegetables, only to be greeted with a present left by the neighborhood cat. The big challenge is that unlike dogs, cats tend to go their own way and they don't take kindly to your efforts to train them or tell what to do (or where to do it). Solve your tabby problem the same way you would dissuade other large animals from helping themselves to your SFG—**use a chicken-wire cage**. If you can't get the cage built right away, there are other effective ways to keep cats away.

That's why a better solution might be a homemade hot pepper spray. Boil a teaspoon of cayenne pepper or hot sauce in 2 quarts of water, let it cool, and fill a spray bottle with the potion. Then just spray around the perimeter of your SFG box. The smell is offensive to cats' delicate noses and can even convince local deer that your SFG isn't worth the trouble. Whatever you do, don't turn to the old gardener's trick of using mothballs to repel cats; the mothballs can be toxic to animals and children.

What can I do to keep my corn crop safe from all the wildlife that want to eat it?

Corn is always a challenge because, well, who doesn't love corn? Certainly squirrels, raccoons, crows, and other wild visitors think it's a tasty treat. But humans love corn, so I had to come up with a foolproof way to grow corn to maturity while keeping it safe and sound. Here's the way to do it. Drive a 6-foot steel fence post outside each corner of your SFG box. First, when you plant your corn seeds

Continued

(soaked for 30 minutes in sun-warmed water), lay a 4 × 4 cover of 1-inch chicken wire on top of the box. Crows love to dig up the seeds or even young sprouts. After the sprouts come through the wire and are about 6 inches tall, all danger is past for now.

Carefully remove the cover and store for later use. When your corn stalks grow to about 4 feet tall, wrap chicken wire (the small kind, with 1-inch holes) around the fence posts. You can buy 30-foot lengths, although some places sell it by the foot and they even cut it for you. Add a roof of the same chicken wire across the top. This will keep the critters out of the corn and will even prevent pesky crows from eating the seeds and seedlings before they have a chance to get growing. Tie the roof to the sides with twist ties so that you can undo them and reach in to harvest the corn. As a bonus, the corn stalks will grow up through the chicken wire, which will help support the stalks as they grow and keep them safe in strong winds. Because the chicken wire is very thin, the pollen from the corn stalks can still drift down and pollinate the ear silk so you get full ear development.

SAFETY FIRST!

Rodents and vermin such as mice, moles, and gophers can all be very unpleasant when they interrupt your nicely tended yard. Many people find them disgusting in general. I can really understand how people get so upset that they just want to use the most powerful solution they can find. Unfortunately, that sometimes leads them to poisons and baits. Rodent baits and poisons do the same thing: they tempt the rodent with a tasty treat, which then causes the rodent to die. The problem is twofold—pets and children can get into poisons, and so can wildlife that you don't want to kill. In addition, nobody wants dead rats or gophers lying around in your yard. Those present a danger to other animals who might consider a dying rodent easy prey. So I'd strongly suggest you look for other means to eliminate any rodents in your garden.

❓ Is there any way to stop raccoons from stealing from my garden?

❗ Raccoons are pretty wily animals and that mask they wear says it all: they are world-class garden thieves. They are also gutsy and more and more commonplace even in suburbs and cities. The first steps to take in making your garden a raccoon-free zone is to **remove all non-garden temptations** that might draw raccoons into your yard. If you know they are a problem in your neighborhood, make sure you have locking lids on your garbage cans, or that the cans are secured in a garage or another structure. Don't leave pet food dishes outside; raccoons are big fans of dog and cat food, and they like pet water bowls as well. Same goes for bird feeders. They'll open them right up for the seeds inside.

Even if there aren't other temptations, raccoons may decide to visit your yard just for all those delicious edibles in your SFG. Of course one of the big advantages to SFG is it can be (and should be) close to your house. If the raccoons are getting into the yard along a fence or other path, spread a border of **moth crystals**. They just hate moth crystals on their paws, and will turn right around when they notice the smell. Sometimes, though, the raccoons will be entering your yard by tree. That's why you should protect your SFG boxes—and particular favorites such as corn plants—with a ring of **blood meal**. The blood meal repulses the raccoons because they absolutely hate the smell.

Lastly, add some motion-activated lights near your SFG and you'll not only cut down on nightly raccoon visits, you'll also send other nocturnal wildlife packing. Of course if you have a lot of four-legged pests, you may want to build an SFG chicken-wire cover for all your boxes. It keeps so many unwanted visitors out—even volleyballs and soccer balls. (May dent but not destroy is what I say!)

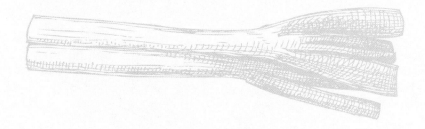

What's the best way to deal with a field mice problem?

Mice—and to a lesser degree, rats—are rarely a problem in an SFG because the box and its contents are elevated—they are more a concern in a row garden. Still, if you have them in your yard, I can see wanting to get rid of them. Controlling vermin like this is a challenge because they are so small and can fit into such tiny spaces. The first line of defense is a clean yard and garden. Mice and rats don't like to be seen. If the aisles are tidy and clean as they are with SFGs, rodents are less likely to want to commute along those paths.

Mulch is another problem. A thick layer of straw or hay mulch is a favorite nesting place for field mice. You'll want to check your mulch for any critters, and you might consider **using a less comfortable mulch**, like coarser chopped-up wood pieces. You have a couple of options for dealing with these vermin head on. The most common solution is a snap trap. These are usually baited with a smear of peanut or a piece of chocolate, and the trap and dead body are just thrown away when you catch the animal (buy the size trap that matches the type of vermin you have). You can also use **glue traps**, which are inexpensive and easy—just bait, and throw away when you catch the mice or rat.

There are a couple problems with these traps in a garden. First, your pets don't know the traps are for vermin, and neither do small children. Handling the dead bodies isn't pleasant either. That's why many people use **live traps**. These have plastic cases with doors inside. The rodent goes in after bait and is trapped inside. Then you release it in the wild, like a state park or large wooded area far from any homes. Of course, you can also turn to the old tried-and-true method of keeping a few cats in the yard. Hopefully, they aren't as lazy as mine and will hunt down any rodents who are trying to steal from your garden.

A simple live trap such as this is the most humane solution to a field mice problem, but keep in mind that it's a lot of work. You're going to have to catch and release more than one critter.

The blue jays in my yard are driving me crazy. How can I stop them?

There's no denying that bigger birds—like blue jays, robins, and crows—can be nuisances. They try to get in and eat your new seedlings. They'll peck out the seeds you just planted and then, of course, when the corn is getting ripe they'll come in and eat it right on the stalk. They can even strip all your sunflowers. The trick is to **cover everything** so that they can't get at it. You'll find netting for just this purpose at most any nursery, large hardware store, and the garden sections of home centers. The netting is just draped over the plants and left there. You can easily reach under to water and work on the garden, but the netting's mesh is fine enough that birds cannot get through it, and they have a hard time holding onto it to work on the plants in the first place.

One extra note here: some of these birds—especially blue jays and crows, can become extremely territorial and aggressive. They have no qualms about dive-bombing pets, children, and gardeners, and can make working on your SFG very unpleasant. If this happens to you, there are a number of solutions you can consider—none work perfectly, but you can usually find one that works for your situation. All involve faking out the birds. Some people swear by **pie tins, or other shiny flat pieces of metal** that you hang from tree branches. There are also fake predators such as plastic horned owls (some even come with movable heads) that you perch on a fence in the yard. Unfortunately, eventually the birds come to realize these are just fake. If the problem is really bad, you may want to invest in one of the predator bird sound systems that scare away the blue jays or crows with the sounds of larger birds like hawks.

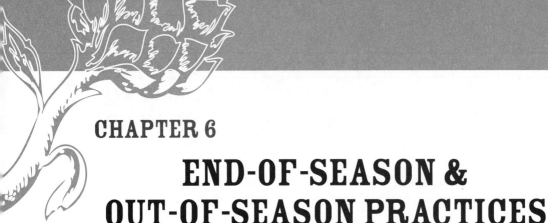

CHAPTER 6

END-OF-SEASON & OUT-OF-SEASON PRACTICES

Winter can be the saddest time in a gardener's year. That lush plot of tasty vegetables dies down and goes quiet, and we all go back to shopping in grocery stores (unless you've been smart enough to grow extra and freeze it). We settle in to longingly look through seed catalogs and page through our favorite gardening books. You find yourself looking out the window thinking, "When is spring going to get here?"

But before you get all cozy in your favorite easy chair in front of a roaring fire, you need to put your SFG boxes to sleep. It's certainly a lot less work than shutting down a row garden, but some basic preparation will ensure that your SFG is ready to go at the earliest possible moment in the new growing season.

Of course, you may also want to extend the growing season on either end. I don't blame you; what could be better than fresh vegetables on the table for Thanksgiving? Or, dare I say it, for Christmas! Keeping the garden going into cold weather, and firing it up long before other gardeners are growing outdoors is one of the most promising benefits of Square Foot Gardening.

No matter what you do with the off-season or end-of-season periods, we at the SFG Foundation inevitably get a lot of questions about how to handle boxes, soil, plants such as perennials and biennials, and more. There are a lot of little details in shutting down the garden or extending the growing season, just as there are during the warm-weather months when your garden is growing like mad.

> *"Just awesome! Before I just couldn't get started with a garden, too overwhelmed . . . you have given me the courage to start. It's all simplified for me."*
>
> —Susan in Arizona

We've taken great pains to answer all those questions because getting the most out of your SFG means making sure it's well taken care of even in the winter.

MEL'S TIP: INDOOR RIPENING

Don't waste those green tomatoes just because the first frost is upon you. You can ripen green tomatoes by putting them inside a paper bag and placing the paper bag in a closed plastic bag. Then store in a cool, dark area such as a cabinet or closet. Check daily to see if the tomatoes have ripened.

How should I winterize my SFG boxes for the harsh weather in my Northeastern location?

It doesn't take much work to put your SFG box to sleep for the cold winter months, and just a few steps will make getting the box up and running next spring a snap. First, let's do a little **"fall" cleaning**. Remove leaf litter and mulch. Then take off your grid if it is removable, and store it in a garage, mudroom, shed or other protected area. "Fluff" your Mel's Mix a bit. Add a little compost, because you'll inevitably have lost a little to wind and just working with your plants. If you want to keep your soil in perfect shape and ready to go for spring, I sometimes suggest that Square Foot Gardeners put their boxes "to sleep," with a **blanket of plastic or landscape fabric** secured down around the box on all sides. In fact, if you choose to do this, you probably won't need to remove the grid. And that's about all you need to close up your SFG boxes for the off-season. After you're done, you'll have a lot of time left over; if you want to be a good Samaritan you can offer to help your neighbor do all that work in shutting down his row garden! They always seem to leave one of their hoes lost under a blanket of weeds never gotten to. Ah, but wait till next spring they say! I couldn't help slipping those comments in, forgive me.

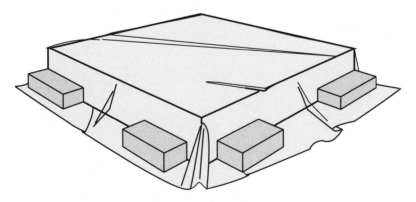

Thick black sheeting not only protects your box from soil loss and infiltration over the winter, it also solarizes the soil, preparing for the next planting season.

MEL'S TIP: SFG FACING FRONT

The off-season is a time to reflect on what has worked—and perhaps, what hasn't—in your SFG. You may be completely happy with your boxes and how much they produced, or you may just see a need for a few changes. If an SFG box was in the way of children playing in the backyard for instance, or if it didn't get quite the amount of sun you thought it would, it might be the perfect time for a change. You also might want to add boxes and increase your harvest. Many times, beginning Square Foot Gardeners find they're ready to take on an additional box or two so that they can put up extra produce, or just to have more on hand for extended family and friends.

Either way, I'd encourage you to look to the front yard. In my experience, gardeners often ignore the possibilities of a sunny front yard. You can have a nice box along a porch featuring both flowers and vegetables, or you could line the driveway or walkway with 2-foot-wide boxes in whatever length works best. If you do decide to add SFG boxes to your front yard, choose your crops carefully. Most people don't have a fenced-in front yard and you don't want your peppers or tomatoes walking off down the street in the hands of some passerby! And you want it so pretty and neat and clean that how could anyone complain. You could also enter our annual Front Yard contest and win yourself a few hundred dollars.

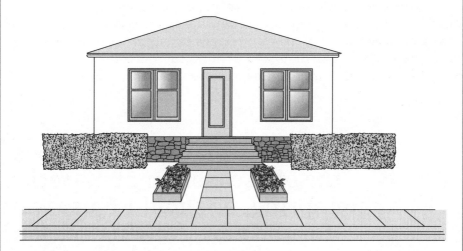

SFG boxes are right at home in the front yard, and can be configured to suit your landscape. Here, two boxes have been adapted to a 2 × 4 shape to run alongside a front walk.

145

How can I determine what my frost date is, and what the growing and harvesting seasons are for my exact location?

Anybody who has ever gardened knows that every location is a little bit different. Your home may be high up or low down in your growing zone, which can create a "microclimate." But no matter where you are, there is a gardening hero and expert for your location, known as the **County Cooperative Extension Service agent**. The Cooperative Extension Service was founded precisely to help local growers—gardeners and farmers alike—by answering questions specific to the region. Local agents are experts on everything from local weather patterns and frost dates, to regional plants and pests and diseases, to the best varieties to grow in your local area. Check in the Yellow Pages or online for your local Cooperative Extension office and use them every chance you get, or they may just go away. And that would be a big loss. Find your local office at the Extension Service's website: www.csrees.usda.gov/Extension. When you talk to them, thank them for all their great service, and all the help they are to gardeners of America.

Can I plant anything over the off-season in preparation for spring, or should I just wait for the new growing season?

Here's something I suggest to Square Foot Gardeners around the country: **grow bulbs!** Bulbs are just a super way to kick off your new gardening season with some beautiful early spring color. Really perk up your boxes with a selection of tulips in all different colors (you can even find some that are nearly black!), daffodils, hyacinths, or the really early snowdrops that might peek out while there's still snow on the ground. You buy and then plant the bulbs in the fall and they rest all winter underground and spring up (get that?) in the spring. That's how you can remember fall versus spring bulbs, which are different.

Early spring bulb plants, like the fantastic display in this SFG box, are delightful ways to start the new season. Once they're planted, they'll come up every year for quite a few years after that, so it's a real good investment. And you can still plant things right over them, because the bulbs are deep down at the bottom of your soil, and your regular garden will fit right over the top of them.

Can't I just leave my old plants in the box at the end of the season? Won't they just compost right in place?

That would sure be nice if it were true. But as much as a SFG saves labor, there are certain things you have to do—and one of them is cleaning out dead plants. Not only does cleaning up your boxes at the end of the season make them look nicer over winter, it helps keep the box healthy. Decaying plant matter can harbor disease and insects. So as soon as the first real frost kills off your plants, **remove them from the box.** Make sure you put everything that isn't diseased right into your compost pile. Chop it up, mix it in.

Mel, I've noticed you always wear a straw hat! Do you change your hat for different seasons, or do you always the same one?

Would it surprise you to know that I have 24 hats? I figure women get to collect shoes, so men should have something for their closets as well. I do change hats for the winter, when I wear a warmer felt hat. Seriously though, I think a hat is pretty much a necessary piece of clothing for any gardener. You can get a lot of sun in a short amount of time without realizing it, so a hat is a great way to protect your skin when you're tending your SFG boxes. And it keeps you cool to boot! You will be out in your SFG planting and caring for it long before your neighbor's row garden soil has dried out enough to start his annual digging and spading and raking and then rototilling his rows. That means you will get the spring sun much sooner than he does, so get a spring hat and enjoy.

Do I need to water my cold-weather or overwintering crops?

You do. Even **cold-weather crops get thirsty**. But here's a trick: don't water them late in the afternoon or the moisture might freeze overnight. If you water in the morning after a chilly night, just imagine it was you out there in the garden; wouldn't you like something warm to drink in the morning? That tells your plants, "Good morning, time to wake up and start growing."

MEL'S TIP: LITTLE SCIENCE WONDERS

Want to give your kids a great science project for school or a science fair? Have them take over one of your 4 × 4 SFG boxes for the winter, and let them see what plants they can grow underneath a warming tent. Try parsley or spinach, or have the kids Google other cold-weather plants. Cover the PVC pipe hoop structure described on page 22 with 6-mil clear plastic, and have blankets ready to throw over the tent at night. Make the cover so that it is still easy to get in and out of the tent (not you, the kids—and not even them—just their hands). Make sure the wind doesn't carry the structure away by weighting down the edges of the plastic or blankets with cinderblocks or bricks (put them in old pillowcases to keep them from tearing the plastic). Have your children measure the temperature inside the tent every day and plot it on a graph. Have them record the amount of the sun the bed receives, how much the plants grow in their winter sanctuary, and measure the harvest. Help them by taking photos along the way. Uh oh, I hear, "You're not going to use my best blankets and pillowcases out in the garden, I don't care how important your science award might be." Okay, let's go to a neighborhood yard sale or swap meet. Lots of linen and blankets for pennies. Well, okay, dollars, but not many. I've done it.

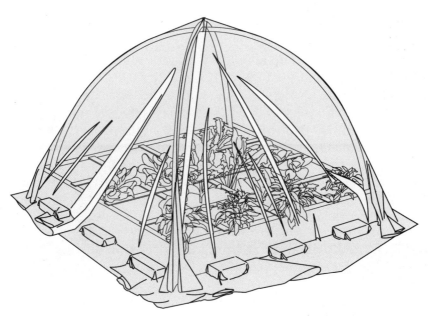

A properly secured plastic tent over an SFG box can be the perfect laboratory for curious kids.

MEL'S STORIES

A WINTER MORNING

Back in the 1980s (I know, many of you were kids then), I managed to get quite a lot of promotion going for my first SFG book, and even got on several TV shows. One of them was an appearance on *Good Morning Boston*, which was pretty good exposure as far as I was concerned. I had to lug a 4 × 4 SFG box with me from the airport, and fill it up with soil and plants for my interview segment, but you can't get better press than a few minutes on TV. I was going to go on after Shelley Winters, the famous actress, probably best remembered for her role in *The Poseidon Adventure*. She was quite the character and was wearing a big fur coat and she kept teasing all the program's staff about what she had on underneath that coat.

I watched from the wings as she gave her interview, which was hilarious and—even though it was early in the morning—everyone was pepped up about it. That set the stage for my interview, and I was glad for all the energy she left behind. They showed my book just like they're supposed to when an author comes on for an interview, and the whole segment went off just about perfect. I got almost six minutes, if I remember correctly, which is a good long time on TV and all in all, things couldn't have gone better. Afterwards, I told people I should have Shelley Winters open for every interview I gave. That usually got a good laugh. The only thing was, I never did find out what she had on (or not) underneath that fur coat!

Is there anything I can do to spruce up my SFG boxes over winter?

Absolutely. There's just no reason at all to allow your SFG boxes to be boring in the off-season. You can start at the Thanksgiving holiday, by staking dried stalks of corn (so they don't fall over) for a nice fall look. Put some oversized pumpkins in as well. Find a few boldly colored sheets or large tablecloths at a yard sale or dollar store, and you've got some great SFG box decorations. Put your chicken-wire cover in place and wrap it with a sheet in the color that suits the holiday—Thanksgiving, Christmas, or even New Year's—and secure the sheet in place down along the sides with a bungee cord. That will hold the sheet tightly in place and make it look really nice.

Even though some gardeners take down their vertical supports in the off season, I like to leave them up because the nylon netting looks gorgeous with a little frost or snow on it. It'll make a beautiful pattern to look at out your kitchen window. You can feed the birds in your yard over winter by slathering a little peanut butter and sunflower seeds over a pine cone, and hanging it from your vertical frame. The birds can sit on the nylon netting without freezing their feet, and they're sure to provide endless hours of entertainment.

You can even put Christmas lights on your vertical SFG support, but please don't use the blinking kind; people would call that a blinking Square Foot Garden and we tend not to like that.

❓ Is there any trick to boosting my harvest right at the end of the season? I've heard there are ways to do that.

❗ Indeed there are. You'll increase your harvest by **watering your summer fruiting plants less than normal during the final weeks of the season**. With the lack of water, the plants will sense that the season is coming to a close and will send all their energy to ripening the fruit that has already been formed. It's simple biology—the plant is in a rush to produce seeds for reproduction the next year! I'm sure glad we're not that way!

❓ What's the best way to get a jump on the new growing season?

❗ You can **start seedlings early**, in a warm sunny place indoors. But I wouldn't go to all the expense of starter trays or other nursery items. Save some money and use toilet paper tubes cut in half or about to 2 inches tall. (I wasn't sure as I was writing this, so I went to measure. Guess how long? Exactly 4½ inches. So in half is perfect. See how many useful and interesting cocktail party things you can learn with SFG?) Fill them with Mel's Mix. Use a marking pen to label each tube with what you're planting and the date and place them in a shallow tray filled with a layer of water. If the tubes begin to unravel, you can always keep them closed with a small rubber band.
Keep the tray in a warm place until the seeds sprout, and then move them into direct sunlight until you plant them in your SFG box.

This is an easy and inexpensive way to start your seedlings out right, and get them ready for transplanting into your SFG box at the first opportunity.

MEL'S TIP: FINAL FRUIT FREE-FOR-ALL

As you approach the end of the season, you want to get the most and best fruit and vegetables possible from your SFG plants before the first frost hits and kills them off. Here's a trick that will give the best harvest at the last moment. To force tomatoes to ripen quickly on the vine, snip off all new blossoms and baby fruit. That will send all the plant's energy to the tomatoes that are left. In addition, picking tomatoes as soon as they turn red will help the plant redirect its energy to completing the growth of more medium-sized tomatoes. These tricks work just as well for peppers and eggplant.

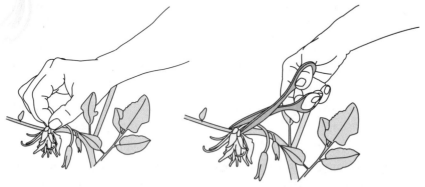

Snipping off suckers and blossoms is a great way to direct the plant's energy into ripening the fruits.

How do I make sure I don't import bugs when I bring plants inside for the winter?

If you're potting up and bringing some of your plants indoors for the winter (plants like lettuce, parsley, and other herbs are ideal for this) you want to make sure you don't bring along hitchhikers with plants. Place the entire plant in a large, clear plastic bag and add a couple of mothballs to the bag (place the bag where children and pets won't get to it). The plants will survive, but after a week or two, any bugs will be dead.

END-OF-SEASON ... OR NOT!

Want a garden all winter? Well, who wouldn't really? Of course, you're probably asking yourself, "How the heck can I garden through the sleet, snow, and freezing temperatures?" Good question, and I've got just the answer for you. If you love gardening and like a bit of a challenge, this may be just the thing for you. Build a greenhouse structure! Yes, I know full-blown greenhouses are expensive. But you can start small, maybe with one that's expandable. It doesn't have to be glass; you can make the panels out of thick plastic that will work almost as well.

Take advantage of the sun by making sure one long wall of the greenhouse faces south. Line the opposite wall with tanks or jugs of water and they will suck up warmth during the day and release it at night, keeping your plants warm and cozy during the chilly evenings without a lot of supplemental heat.

You can build a greenhouse against a garage wall or house foundation wall, which might aid in keeping the temperature warm. One year in Long Island, New York, moving into a new house, I found a way to take advantage of natural heating. I dug down 3 feet and built my greenhouse into the ground. That did two things. First, it limited the glass I needed to use (I built a brick foundation). That helped keep the temperature higher in the winter and cooler in the summer just like a cave in the ground.

All right, let's suppose you can't afford a greenhouse, even a makeshift one. You can build the SFG version of a 3 × 6 foot cold frame, as I did one winter. Rather than build the usual wooden sloping sides and go to the trouble of cutting plywood at an angle, I dug down about a foot and created a sloped bed that faced the sun. I created a berm all the way around with the soil I removed. Then I put a couple inches of sand in the bottom, and laid a heating coil (you can find these at home centers and hardware stores) along the bottom and ran it up to a plug and a thermostat. I ran an extension cord out from the

garage to the plug, then made a watertight connection for the connection plug. I kept the temperature between 50°F and 60°F, which conserved electricity but still kept the plants warm. I covered the wires with a little more sand, laid down a weed fabric, and put down 4 inches of compost, topped with 4 inches of Mel's Mix. So I had 8 inches of growing soil.

I laid out my squares, put down a grid, and started planting. Then I installed the box around the hole in the ground, the box consisted of a bottomless 3-foot × 6-foot box made from 2 × 6 lumber, two stories high. It lay right on the sloping bottom so the sides as well as the bottom were sloping toward the southern winter sun.

Of course you need a top over the cold frame, so I laid a large storm window frame across the wood sides. It kept the plants toasty, and I could easily move it to water, tend, and harvest my crops or let a little heat out if things were too hot.

CHAPTER 7

MAKING A DIFFERENCE WITH SFG

I'm not shy about challenging gardeners to get involved, whether that means starting a community garden, teaching SFG, or running a business around it—the SFG method is the ideal tool for any of those challenges. But believe me, I know firsthand how much work a community garden entails and how dedicated you have to be to start and run one here or abroad (much less teaching SFG, or earning money from it). I also know the reward those things promise. A successful community garden, in particular, boosts pride, creates a huge sense of accomplishment, and feeds many, many people. I think anyone who has ever done it would say it's well worth the effort. I know it was for me; I developed Square Foot Gardening out of my experience with a community garden back in 1975-77!

Dealing with all the different people necessary to keep a community garden humming along can be one of the biggest hurdles a community garden organizer faces. Then there's the day-to-day maintenance of the garden, which presents its own set of trials and tribulations. Along the way, there's no end to the questions that can pop up.

But an even bigger challenge is to bring SFG to the rest of the world. As much as an SFG community garden can benefit any suburban community or an impoverished inner city neighborhood, it can literally transform the lives of the Third World poor who are struggling with bare subsistence. No matter where it is, a community garden is a wonderful and complicated project that comes with many puzzling issues. I've tried to address those issues in this chapter.

Yes, community gardens are a terrific way to get involved in your neighborhood, town, city, or the world beyond. But there is another fantastic SFG way to get involved and have a big impact: Become a Certified Square Foot Gardening teacher/instructor.

It might not be everybody's cup of tea, but if you have the time and you love SFG as much as I do (and see the fantastic world-changing aspects of it as most people do), you can jump right in and spread the word. If you're interested in becoming a certified member of the SFG Foundation, go to our website and see the several ways you can become qualified: home study, online and in person at any of our three-day symposiums held around the country. We even held one in Hawaii (hey that's a state, and a darn good one for growing gardens).

I spend a lot of my time with my SFG teacher/instructors, and I know the issues they face and some of the puzzling questions they field. I try to help them figure out the best ways to help their students. And that's the goal for the questions I've chosen to highlight in the second half of this chapter.

"I want to be the heart and soul of Square Foot Gardening. I want to teach SFG to others throughout the USA and the world—not only for their personal benefit but also for humanitarian purposes. In essence, I want to make a difference to as many 'starfish' as possible by guiding others to learn this superb method of gardening. I want to continue the legacy!"

—Karen B. from Utah

Lastly, we've provided guidance here on expanding SFG as a commercial enterprise. I like to see people make money with SFG because it means they are bringing more healthy, organic produce into the world, and it is just another way to get exposure for this innovative gardening method.

So I think you'll find answers to every issue that's perplexed you, whether you've tried to get an SFG community garden off the ground, or are trying to educate a whole new crop of Square Foot Gardeners!

❓ I've heard you talk a lot about using SFG to solve world hunger, but where would you actually begin?

❗ You're right, I've talked a lot about how SFG can be the answer to world hunger, and I truly believe that. I have studied it extensively. I believe it would have to start with tough love. First, stop feeding people; just stop giving them free food. Tell them that's it, no more. Hereafter, we'll show you how to grow your own food, and then you can show your children how, and they can teach their children how.

Of course it can't be a simple just stop and go, there has to be a reasonable transition period and I know some of your letters are going to talk about what some call the "bleeding heart" approach: "Oh what about the infirmed, elderly, homeless, too young, too old, etc." Once you say, "If you think you are needy, come in and we will feed you, no questions asked and we won't even ask you to help clean up and wash your dishes, we have lots of people that will do that for you. Our volunteers want something to do to make them feel good about themselves," and I think the current phrase is giving something back. How do you stop that whole scenario? You can't and then we all are in trouble.

Well the answer is those whom we teach how to grow their own food will grow a little extra for those who absolutely cannot. That means the hungry will help the hungry. Is that cruel and heartless? NO, absolutely not. That's called tough love at its finest. Some would even say it's about time the needy helped the needy and then ALL could become non-needy. Is that a word? In this country, we have plenty of space to dedicate to these Grow Your Own community gardens. You can put one behind a library (with SFG books and videos right inside the library for anyone to check out), in a church parking lot, a vacant city lot, on a school field, next to a police or fire station, or anywhere there are wide open, unused public lands (heck, even in the corner of a park or public ball field). Then we supply the materials needed: the boxes, Mel's Mix, grids and seeds.

We can train volunteer Master Gardeners to teach the method to all newcomers, and maybe we can get all the Garden Writers to stop teaching single row gardening and come in as elite writers and teachers that they are to oversee this tremendous project.

The County Cooperative Extension Service agent can be the center of information and administration. Wait a minute, most people don't want the government to start and administer any more programs. That would get Congress involved and they have taken plenty of abuse lately. Let's just let the people organize and run this. Maybe all the churches or nonprofit and humanitarian organizations could be trusted to run a healthy and non-wasteful operation. Hey I know one we can trust to have the knowledge and smarts to do all that. The Square Foot Gardening Foundation. We would be honored to train any experts we need for these gardens. I just don't believe anybody wants to take handouts of food. Why would they? Why would they want to stand in line for hours and be humiliated, when they could tend a garden in less time and enjoy the dignity of raising their own food?

I really believe we've got everything we need to solve world hunger, we just need to be willing to put SFG into action, first countrywide and then share with the rest of the world. Would our country regain its respect and acknowledgement again if we did something like this? How long would it take? I think in 10 years it would be a huge success.

HIGH-RISE HOMESTEADING

We at the Square Foot Gardening Foundation are always interested in how SFG could be used to feed great numbers of people, so I really perked up when I received a letter from a think tank in Washington, D.C., saying that the question had come up about how many people SFG could feed. One source had estimated that an acre of gardens could feed 5,000 people! The people at the think tank thought that number was wildly inflated, and wanted my input to determine what the actual number might be.

As a retired engineer, I thought that was a pretty interesting problem to work out. I did some figuring, then designed a way to double the harvest from our SFG system and set out to calculate just how many SFG boxes would fit in an acre of land. I envisioned it as a miniature one-acre farm without rows or tractors. It would have its own composting operation, and I pictured it in some tropical country in the Third World, operating 12 months out of the year. I called this "High-Rise Homesteading," because the garden would be built with two different levels; 4 × 12 boxes on the ground, with steel fence posts driven into the ground every 4 feet on both sides of each box and another 4 × 12 box with a plywood bottom suspended 5 feet high right over the bottom one. So there would be two levels—a double-decker design—giving twice as much harvest per square foot.

In the end, using all this space, I calculated we could feed 500, not 5,000, people. But still, that's quite a lot of people. Even better, I figured that 50 people could be employed at minimum wage, maintaining and harvesting the garden. Now think of that. No tractors or gas-guzzling noisy machines or trucks, all organic, no fertilizer, or pesticides or insecticides, all hand labor, no tools or digging required, only 10 percent of the water needed.

That leaves the big question: Why aren't we doing this all around the world? Heck, Mr. President, members of

Congress, why aren't we doing this in our own country? Instead of paying people not to garden, paying people not to work, collecting donated food, then making the hungry or poor stand in long lines around the corner to get this free food. If you come up with the answer to that one, let me know.

A double-decker SFG box design such as this would effectively double the yield in an acre "High-Rise Homestead" garden.

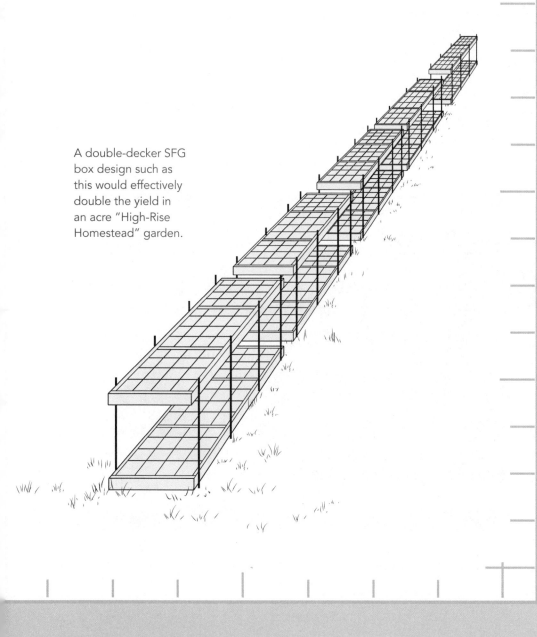

Want to change the world? Me too. That's why I've worked hard to spread the word of SFG around the globe (although, we call if Square Metre Garden outside America's borders, it's exactly the same as SFG). I have spoken in front of an audience of agronomy and agricultural professors at the University of El Salvador as part of the SFG Foundation's efforts in initiating a countrywide composting and gardening program. I've traveled to India, Britain, Haiti, all over Central and South America, Nepal, Thailand, Latin America, of course to our good neighbors in Canada and Mexico, and even to Scandinavia teaching people about Square Metre Gardening. Everywhere I've gone,

This SFG box is used to train gardeners in El Salvador. The SFG method is helping impoverished people in that country fend for themselves.

the natives get it right away. They understand that SFG is a way to feed their families, be healthy, become independent and even make a little money.

A while back I received a letter from a woman who had recently graduated from Redland College in California. She had gone on a mission to Africa, organized by her environmental professor, with no agenda but to go village to village to see how the students could help out. It was sort of a hit-or-miss effort. She was writing to let me know that she was forming a non-profit to redo the trip, featuring SFG as the center point. It dawned on me that every college must have trips like this, and wouldn't it be great if service organizations like Rotary, the Lions Club, or even college alumni groups adopted this project. We could send college students out into villages all over the world to become teachers of SFG and leaders of self-sufficiency. They would leave behind them the ability for the people to become healthy and self-sufficient. No other program in existence does that. Let's teach self-sufficiency instead of just asking how can we help you. Let's really help others not by giving them free food for a day or free shoes for a year, but a lifetime of information and a method that will keep them healthy and well fed, all by themselves.

So I say, if you've got the travel bug, why not take SFG with you on your travels? Starting a community garden can be an amazingly rewarding experience, but starting one overseas, or helping a Third-World community start their own, can be even more amazing and rewarding! Write us today, and tell us how you can help. Go there or help us help others. I'll end this with a song, do you remember: "Not for an hour, not for day, but always."

SFG & SOLVING WORLD HUNGER:
AN INTERVIEW WITH MEL

Q: Can we solve world hunger?

Mel: I think we have the answer right here, right now, in SFG.
It's so simple, you can teach it from pictures.

Q: What's at the core of world hunger? Why is it such an
intractable problem?

Mel: Up until now, I think the world's solution to hunger has
been to "give a man a fish," instead of "teaching him how
to fish." We do have excess, and we can keep giving to the
hungry but that doesn't actually solve the problem. The
problem just goes on, and the world's hungry are dependent
on everyone else rather than controlling their own fates.

Q: What about other solutions? What about aid programs?

Mel: Even when we try to help the poor and hungry in the
Third World, we try to help them with First-World solutions.
The answer has been to go into a poor country and teach
them how to do our method of agriculture. We send them
genetically engineered seeds to produce more crops. We give
them better fertilizers all the time, to improve their yield
from their meager soil and land. We convince them that they
need the finest machinery like what we have, and that they
should plow up the land, as little as they have and as poor
the soil is, enrich it with fertilizers they can't really afford,
and plant all those crops that we do. That's our solution.
It worked for us didn't it? Why shouldn't it work for them?
Only we've done that for a zillion years and we're still doing
it and it's still not working. No matter how much we help
the farmer, the people are still poor and can't afford the
food, no matter how much there is.

Q: So why SFG? How can it solve world hunger?

Mel: Well, the big problem is that in a Third World country,
they don't have the money, the knowledge, the experience,

the land . . . they basically don't have anything! And we keep trying to teach them the old-fashioned single row method. That's no good. It's wasteful, harmful, and at odds with the environment. But now, Square Foot Gardening is easily converted to Square Metre Gardening and has been proven to work anywhere in the world. We teach a woman to garden and then she teaches her children. She needs very little space and no machinery. No fertilizer is needed, no tools are needed, no skills are needed, no knowledge is needed. Just a few regular old-fashioned seeds, 10 percent of the water a Victory Garden would need, and we produce 100 percent of the harvest. It just doesn't matter what their soil is like because we don't use it. They make compost to grow in. It is that simple and uncomplicated.

Q: So you honestly think SFG could actually solve world hunger?
Mel: I don't think, I know. It's not a matter of could it, but how long it would take.

Q: How long would it take?
Mel: With the right commitment, not long. I believe we could do it in 10 years, with an investment of around $1 billion. Then that would be it, solved forever! But I think it's also about much more than just hunger. SFG is also about how to be healthy, happy, and non-hungry. The Square Foot Gardening Foundation believes that EVERYONE in the world can learn to grow pretty much all of their own food in a very small space. Doesn't matter where they live, what conditions they live in, what their land is like, or what their circumstances are. Why, we can even put a SFG on wheels if they're a nomad. I hope people keep an open mind, lobby for SFG and who knows? Maybe someone in power will say "we could do this," and we can! And we will!

Does starting a community garden mean I have to find someone who owns a plot of land?

It sure would be nice if folks who own a vacant lot would just contribute it to the cause, but that's rarely the case. More often, you need to get a commitment from a municipality for land that is underused, like one corner of a park, playground, a mixed-use area, or even a vacant lot that the city hasn't yet decided how they will use. You can also talk to your local schools and churches. They may have a small bit of land that you can fence off and lay out for the garden. It doesn't take much; remember SFG can do the same job as a Victory Garden but in only 20 percent of the space. You may even be able to tie in the garden with school or church programs!

Are there special features I should consider in planning my community garden?

The basic layout of a SFG community garden is mostly a matter of math—giving each gardener the right amount of space to place their boxes with aisles around them. But beyond that requirement, there are several other features that can improve the garden. The first that comes to mind is a good fence around the entire garden. You remember that old saying, "Fences make for good neighbors?" Well, that's the idea here. You want to keep out stray animals, and those few stray humans that might want to vandalize something like a community garden. I also recommend that a community garden have a nice, shaded sitting area where people can just sit and enjoy their garden, or brag about how big their zucchini are. Remember to add a compost pile and maybe a trash can for general, non-compostable trash.

How do you start a Square Metre Garden overseas?

We've learned that you have to start small and manageable. We also learned you have to start with a woman, the mother of the family. Write me if you want to know why not the man. We ask each woman if she would like to improve her children's nutrition by learning a simple and efficient gardening method called Square Metre Gardening. Okay, okay, I'll tell you why not the man. Because a woman will ask, "How do I do it?" A man will ask, "What's in it for me?" I KNOW, because I've been all over the world and this is exactly the dialog I get. Please don't write me, men, I'm on your side but I want this to work.

We begin by teaching her and her children how to make compost from all the things people throw away, which helps clean up the environment and makes the whole neighborhood look a little nicer. Then we start them off with just one Square Metre Garden (essentially, a 3- × 3-foot box), which is divided into nine squares, featuring nine different nutritious crops, such as parsley, chives, beets, Swiss chard, and perhaps some marigolds. All the easy-to-grow, constant-harvest type of plants.

Once they learn the method and her first box is successful, the mother can start a second and a third. The boxes can be built out of local scrap lumber and the soil will be the compost the family is constantly making. So everything is FREE. She may even start growing a cash crop—beyond what she needs to feed her family. And best of all, she can soon start selling the extra compost, a much sought-out super material by any and all gardeners, anywhere in the world.

SFG COMMUNITY GARDENS—THE DO'S AND DON'TS

In the last 25 years, I have organized, run, visited, filmed and observed community gardens all around the country. As you might expect, they all seem to struggle with similar problems and pitfalls. I hate to see gardeners' good intentions go to waste, so of course I had to come up with some very simple guidelines of what to do and, more importantly, what not to do in establishing a community garden.

DON'T . . .

1. **Give too much space to any individual gardener.** This is the biggest mistake I see in community gardens. The illustration on the next page shows what I think is about the best and most area any one gardener or family should tackle. People sometimes get excited and want to grow a whole lot more because they don't understand that you're getting 100 percent of the harvest in 20 percent of the space a row garden takes. All any gardener really needs is about 15 × 15 feet, which will produce plenty of vegetables for an entire family. So limit each gardener's exposure to a reasonable harvest of about 15 × 15 feet, and everyone will be happy you did.

2. **Allow row crops.** SFGs are designed to be super efficient—to provide the maximum harvest in the minimum amount space. Row gardening will disrupt the setup and layout of SFG boxes and the two really can't exist side by side. I know it sounds a little bit strict to say that an SFG community garden is an all-or-nothing proposition, but that's the way it is.

DO . . .

1. **Post the rules.** Might sound a little stuffy, but it's for everyone's benefit. These are usually pretty self-explanatory and with just a little thought, you can come up with a commonsense list that won't get anybody's ire up. Include obvious issues like hours, accessibility, any plants that you want to keep out because they are too messy or invasive, how

conflicts will be settled, and how, where, and what tools will be kept in the garden (you won't need many; remember this is SFG!). This whole list is just a matter of fostering respect for each other's space and efforts. Kind of like a little neighborhood isn't it?

2. **Space aisles correctly.** Check the illustration for what I've found is just about the perfect spacing between boxes and aisles. This 15-foot × 15-foot spacing allows a 2-foot wide path all around the perimeter of each space, with 3 feet between boxes in any one group. If your neighbor has the same thing, then you have created a 4-foot wide path or really nice buffer zone between neighboring family plots. No one should be able to put up a fence, although vertical frames or towers, tripods, and beanpoles should be allowed inside each 4 × 4 planting block. This spacing also eliminates any problems from prolific crops like corn, squash, and pumpkins that might otherwise shade or invade your neighbors' plots. All plants must be contained within each 4 × 4 planting block.

These are standard measurements for the SFG boxes in one corner of a community garden. The measurements are optimal, but can be altered slightly to suit the particular circumstances of your community garden. Keep in mind that the boxes may be reshaped to accommodate an oddly shaped lot. For instance, rather than 4 × 4 feet, a box might be 2 × 8 feet, or two 4 × 4 foot boxes can be turned into a 4 × 8 foot box.

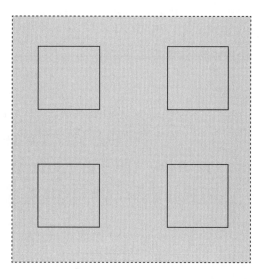

? I think my town could really use a community garden, but I really don't know where to start. Any ideas?

! I sure do have some ideas. I think it's always wise to begin by getting the people who can help you into your corner. Reach out to your mayor, city councilperson, and County Cooperative Extension Service agents and

Master Gardeners. As you get the word out, chances are that someone may already have done some thinking about possible sites and other resources. If you have a local gardening or nature non-profit, set up a meeting. Same goes for agricultural programs through local universities. These people may be able to lead you to grants that will help you in establishing your community garden. Those are the best first steps you can take: making relationships, gathering information and developing resources.

MEL'S MANTRA

Mel believes that all you need is faith and hope!

What we plant
is what will grow.

What we feed
is what will bloom.

What we ignore
will wither and die.

1. Declare your destiny
2. Chart your course
3. Endure and persevere till the end
4. Once in a lifetime—along comes
   a chance,
   a person,
   an opportunity.
   Don't waste it!

A COMMUNITY SUCCESS STORY

Even though I deal with a lot of community gardens and enthusiastic Square Foot Gardeners, sometimes I come across situations that hit home and let me know just how much the world needs SFG. In March of 2011, the Square Foot Gardening Foundation, under our CEO Victoria's direction, was asked to host a three-day symposium to train new volunteers to become certified SFG instructors at the University of South Carolina in Columbia. As Victoria relates it, we met on the USC campus in a campus quad, and during the symposium we discovered that our invitation with the university had been because they were working with an organization called Homeless Helping Homeless (HHH). They had just persuaded the city of Columbia to donate a vacant corner lot where three homes had once stood. The lot had been taken over by drug dealers, and it was a desolate plot of land in a desperate neighborhood.

I'm pretty much a glass-half-full type of person, but even I found it hard to believe that a community garden could succeed in that blighted area. Just the same, we took a field trip to the lot on the third day of the symposium so that everyone could build and plant in the garden. We all went home feeling better about the project.

Fast forward a month, and HHH asked us back for ribbon-cutting ceremony. I think my jaw hit the ground when we pulled up to the lot—it was filled with a beautiful, lush garden that contained SFG boxes for both adults and children. The TV cameras were there to record the ribbon-cutting event and even Mayor Stephen Benjamin showed up and planted his own SFG box (mayors like fresh, delicious vegetables too, you know). I was touched to realize that there would be healthy food and a positive experience for area residents who lacked the transportation to a grocery store. The garden would also serve as a community center—there was a shaded sitting area where neighbors could relax and chat, and lots of space for children to learn and appreciate growing their own food.

The Columbia Community Gardens are an example of many different organizations working together for the common good.

Talking with the residents of the area and listening to people's stories that day made me realize more than ever how the SFG Foundation had, as its primary goal, ending hunger through gardening. And community gardens are the perfect tool to get to that goal. One of the biggest added experiences was that all the neighbors took on the wonderful attitude of this is our garden and we want no more drug dealers or gangs hanging out. And guess what, folks? That's what actually happened. The corner is cleaned of all the bad things of an inner-city slum area. The mayor has asked Victoria to now work with the city and install community SFGs in every one of the city's 24 parks.

Okay, mayors and residents of other big cities, who is next? Send us an invitation and we'll have Victoria and her city park SFG staff experts there the next week, ready to help clean up your city neighborhoods with Square Foot Gardens!

How can I prevent vandalism in my community garden?

I've found that vandalism isn't as much a problem as you might think, but I know people can get discouraged when it happens in a community garden. Nobody wants to show up to their garden only to find plants dug up or stomped down and the garden a mess. Start by making sure everyone in the neighborhood knows what the garden is about. Put up large sign announcing that it is a community garden serving the neighborhood. Of course, fences make good neighbors in any case, and no more so than with a community garden where they will keep out stray dogs as well as potential vandals.

On the same note, you can plant thorny plants along the edges of the garden, although I think this is usually detracts from the garden and doesn't provide enough of a barrier to individuals set on damaging the garden.

Lastly, you can alert the neighborhood watch or residents whose homes overlook the garden to keep their eyes peeled for any problems in the garden. It's always a good idea to get as many people as possible involved in a community garden, even if they aren't doing the gardening themselves!

What pitfalls should I look to avoid in starting a community garden?

I think the number-one problem most people encounter when they jump into the project of starting a community garden is overreaching. It can be real easy to envision a gigantic garden full of delicious, ripe crops, but are you ready for that? It's not only the work, but what are you going to do with your harvest? It would just be silly to grow a huge amount of fruits and vegetables only to find that you don't know how to get them into the hands of people who need them.

Where you would suggest is the best place to set up a community garden in a small city?

Community gardens have so much to offer that I think they should be placed where they'll do the most good. That usually means in a poorer part of town, or wherever access to fresh and healthy vegetables is limited. It's best to choose a location that is as central as possible, ideally near public transportation so that everyone who wants to can visit the garden as often as they like. If you can find a spot close to the inner city, people who might not otherwise be able to eat fresh vegetables will be able to walk a short a distance and pick their own dinner. What a treat! And what a health benefit. Yes, that is a challenge, but that is where it should be.

Inner-city community gardens are some of the most powerful, bringing healthy nutrition, exercise, and hope to lower-income inner city populations.

? Do you know of any grants available for community gardens?

! We can all use a little help in setting up our community gardens, and thank goodness, there are a lot of places to turn for that help. You'll find two basic types of grants: those that award funds to be used as described in the grant application, and those that provide materials such as seeds for the actual garden. Some sources offer both types of assistance. Here's a short list of grants you can apply for.

- America the Beautiful Fund (www.america-the-beautiful.org/free_seeds/index.php) supplies grants of seeds.

- The Lorrie Otto Seeds for Education Grant Program (www.wildones.org/seedmony.htm) provides modest monetary grants to non-profits with an educational component. If your SFG community garden is set up to teach children about SFG, it may qualify.

- The National Gardening Association (www.kidsgardening.org/grants-and-awards) provides thousands of grants through their Kids Gardening program. Grants are awarded to projects in keeping with "NGA's vision of a greener future and belief in the powerful impact gardening programs can have on the mental, physical, and psychological health of individuals."

- Stonyfield Farms (www.stonyfield.com/about-us/our-mission/profits-planet/apply-pfp-grant) provides monetary and product grants for projects that contain an explicit organic or climate change purpose.

- Seeds of Change (www.seedsofchange.com/donations/growingminds.aspx) makes seeds available to programs with an educational component—especially through school-based gardens—through their program called Sowing Millions, Growing Minds.

- The Captain Planet Foundation (www.captainplanetfoundation.org) provides thousands of grants each year, with funding ranging from a few hundred to a few thousand dollars. Specifically, they fund hands-on environmental projects that teach children about the environment and empower today's youth.

- Ashoka's Youth Venture (www.genv.net) funds youth projects founded and driven by teens. The organization focuses on funds for sustainable projects; this can be a great way to get teens involved and to teach them entrepreneurial practices and approaches to non-profit ventures.

MEL'S STORIES

St. John's Baptist Church in Columbia, South
Carolina, has a food pantry that hands out hundreds of
pounds of food every week, in partnership with a local
food bank, Columbia Harvest Hope. St. John's had a
community garden—a row garden full of weeds and
very neglected. At the same time, Columbia College had
been working on a community project to fight Type II diabetes.
Their program involved a model for health awareness, including
a walking program, a crockpot cooking program, and a gardening
element. The idea was that these three components would serve to
teach people about their disease and to be proactive in managing
it—as well as any health problem—rather than turning only to
prescription drugs. St. John's, Columbia College and the Square
Foot Gardening Foundation joined forces to realize the third
(gardening) leg of the program with a 10-box SFG created in
one weekend in an empty lot on church property. The garden is
flourishing with organic fruits, vegetables, herbs, and flowers. It's
a great example of how different elements within the community—
in this case, a church, a college, and a non-profit—can come
together and create a valuable asset in a community garden.

Should we make our own Mel's Mix for our community garden, or purchase prepared Mel's Mix?

That all comes down to how much time and manpower you have, as well as local resources. If your community garden is simply too far from any nursery source or even a large home center, it's going to be very difficult to get enough of the three components to make all the Mel's Mix you need. In that case, I'd recommend ordering premade Mel's Mix, and having it delivered. You might also want to go this route if you simply don't have a lot of strong arms on your community garden team to mix all the Mel's Mix for the individual boxes. However, when possible, I like to see people mix their own, because after building their boxes, it's the first sense people get of really working with something organic and growing their own garden. They also get to touch and feel the components as a learning experience and to help them appreciate the mix.

SAFETY FIRST!

These days, people worry about liability in everything they do—and with good reason. There are more lawsuits being filed today than ever before. That's why it's smart to secure insurance for your community garden if the plot is not already covered by the owner's policy. All you need is a general liability policy to cover any injuries sustained in the garden. Check with local insurance brokers who represent many different insurance companies and can find you the best deal. Also figure in this cost when you're planning the garden rent schedule and applying for grants. Yes! You're going to charge rent. I don't care if it's for the homeless, the needy, or the hungry. If they don't pay a nominal amount to rent their box in the community garden, they're likely not to take care of it. Anyone everywhere can come up with a dollar a month, or $5 for the whole season.

Almost every time I teach an SFG course, someone comes back later and says "I followed your instructions but it didn't work for me." Am I doing something wrong?

I think you should worry if the whole class comes back with the same complaint. But we've found in our experience training gardeners and teaching people the SFG method, that when they say they followed the directions and it didn't work, it's usually the case that they didn't really follow the directions. Sometimes they located the box right under a tree. Another time, they might have used just one, nutrient-poor type of compost in their Mel's Mix rather than five different types. The key is to ask the person the right questions.

If you have them walk you through the process, you'll usually detect right where they went wrong. It's just a matter of asking the specific questions to track down where the process went awry. The most prevalent "how did I go wrong," is with the soil mix. I have had beginners say, "Oh the nursery said I didn't need all those different kinds of composts; he has a great mixed one he could sell me for only $25 a truckload." Or, "I got five kinds of manure from pig, cow, horse, rabbit, and steer. Is that enough?" They are all manures—that's one source but a good one.

Can SFG students learn more about SFG through County Extension Service agents and offices?

Unfortunately, no. The government still doesn't recognize SFG as a viable horticultural method. They've been teaching row gardening for so long that the Department of Agriculture and the County Extension Service don't even list SFG as a method of growing crops. We've heard that some innovative Extension Service agents are teaching it, or at least mentioning it, but the change has to come down from the top.

Government bureaucracies can become mighty entrenched, and I think they just can't get their head around the benefits of SFG. They didn't think it up so it must not be worth anything and to prove their point, they don't teach it in the agricultural colleges. However, some small changes are coming. But you will be as old as I am before they wake up. Just because SFG has been around for going on 40 years, is the biggest selling garden book in history (over 2 million sold so far), was a top-rated TV show in its time, is simple and easy, can be learned from three pictures, requires no tools, no fertilizer, is all organic, needs only 20 percent of the space, 10 percent of the water, 5 percent of the work, 2 percent of the seeds, and there are no weeds, is apparently not justification enough for the gardening corporations and industry to tell you about it.

Can I make money from my training in SFG?

You betcha. Once you become certified, there are many different ways you can earn money with SFG. You can get paid for teaching, consulting, doing workshops, tending other people's gardens, and even selling garden products—you can buy all the products from the SFG Foundation wholesale and sell them retail. A lot of people have done just that!

? Do you have an example of someone who has made a business out of SFG?

! I have several. One of the best was one of our certified instructors who decided to do something new with her expertise. She figured out that there were a lot of people who were probably very open to the idea of SFG, but who didn't want to shop for all the materials, build all the boxes, mix the soil, etc. So she started a business that she described as "Gardens to Go." She sells boxes, Mel's Mix, grids, the whole bit. She will also install the garden. But here's the best part: it's a family affair. She's gotten her teenagers involved and they're learning for the first time about how to work for somebody, how to manage money, and how to spend and invest wisely. She advertises, gives free lectures, and passes out her business brochures. People buy any number of boxes, sometimes pick them up, but often ask her to install them. She grabs her kids, loads up the van, and brings everything she needs to set up the garden.

And while she and the kids are setting up the garden, she primes them on how to SFG so they get off to a great start. On the backend, she offers to take care of gardens when people go on vacations or just can't tend to them. It's a great business model that I can see working all across the country.

? If I wanted to sell some of my SFG crops, what vegetables sell best?

! Tomatoes, without a doubt. Everyone wants homegrown, ripe tomatoes. They're tasty, nutritious, and organic. Corn, on the other hand, is just about the worst crop to grow for money. To estimate how profitable a crop is, you simply have to consider how long it takes to grow, what it's worth on delivery, and how much you can grow in a square foot. Looking at it that way, the best vegetable is almost always radishes. Why? Because you can grow 16 of them in

Continued

one month in 1 square foot and, if they're 10 cents apiece, that's $1.60 times six months of growing season, or about $10 from a single vegetable. Parsley is another good one because you can harvest it continually: once it's half grown you start picking the outer leaves, and continue doing that all season long. It's a matter of logic, really. Back to the corn. I just bought three ears yesterday from my grocery store, at a cost of three for $1. In an SFG you can plant four corn plants per square feet and it takes four months to harvest. So four times 33 cents, or $1.35 for ⅔ of a growing season. Even if it was $6 a dozen, that's still only $2. For all that work and time. See the difference? It's a matter of logic, really.

? How can I become a SFG instructor if I can't make it to one of the three-day symposiums?

! I am sorry you can't make one of our three-day symposiums, because they're a chance to meet many other SFG enthusiasts from all over the country. They form a class to work and motivate each other later. We have held symposiums in many different states, including Utah, Texas, California, Hawaii, Vermont, North Carolina, West Virginia, South Carolina, Illinois, Florida, and several places in Canada. We realized pretty early on that a lot of people might have a hard time making it to the in-person training

A class of newly certified SFG teachers at our former Eden, Utah, location. Don't they look proud?

sessions, so we offer an at-home kit you can order right off our website (www.squarefootgardening.org). Check the site often because we are also developing a brand new certification over the Internet!

? How can I sell the produce I grow?

Early on, I investigated how Square Foot Gardeners could best sell their extra produce. Now, I thought like many people do, maybe a roadside stand. But you have to take into account all that traffic, and you need parking, and maybe the local officials and police department become involved. It could be a real headache and a lot of work just to make it through the red tape. Then I investigated the farmers' market but that took a good part of Saturday and, if you didn't sell it all (and you never do), the rest is too wilted so that was lost.

I also investigated a new idea back then called conscription, where people buy shares in what you raise. It wasn't profitable enough. So I figured there had to be a brand new market, and I found one. I took a huge basket of fresh picked salad fixings—this was in the summer—and I went to the most expensive restaurant in town. I sat down with the chef and the owner and said, "How would you like to have homegrown organic groceries delivered right to your back door every week?" They jumped at the opportunity, even after I told them that the produce would be expensive, because they knew they could put "locally grown" and "organic" right there on the menu. Organic produce is about 20 to 40 percent more expensive than regular and also about 40 percent higher than grocery store prices, but those restaurant professionals knew that it would sell and, anyhow, they make their money off the protein on the plate, not the vegetables. So we made a nice contract, easy as pie.

? What would be a science SFG project for kids of varying ages in my daughter's school?

! Kids will get a big kick of rooting tomato plant suckers (side branches) that you cut off the tomato plants in your SFG. The project is also a great opportunity to teach propagation and how plants grow roots. The project will take about four weeks front to back, and here's what you'll need:

Two large cups, one filled with water, one filled with vermiculite

one pair of scissors

Prune the suckers off the tomato plant and set the cut end down in the water, and one in the vermiculite (which should be kept moist).

Keep the cuttings in a sunny warm location like a south-facing windowsill. Once a week, have the kids carefully remove the suckers to observe and measure root growth and take photos. Then have them chart the root growth in each medium to see which works better, and to identify any other differences. You should have a room full of SFG gardeners before the project is over!

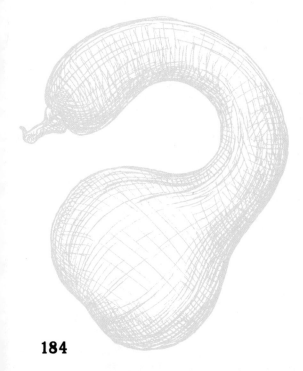

Any suggestions for how I can help my students understand seed spacing and planting?

Sometimes there's nothing like good old memorization and practice, practice, practice. One solution we've had a lot of success with is to drill students on seed spacing. We use a set of flashcards. Have you ever seen them? You can make your own out of 1-foot-square pieces of cardboard or posterboard. Just draw the different seed spacing by marking each spot with a big dot on the cards: 1, 4, 9, and 16. Show them how to the "zip, zap, and bing, bing, bing," because that's a simple and easy learning device. Then have them practice placing seeds, pinch by pinch.

The students should practice with different kinds of seeds in all different shapes and sizes. Once they're working in the garden, it's so easy to drop in what you think is a pinch, but turns out to be five or even 10 seeds. The students can also practice their seed pinches over a piece of white paper until they get the hang of it. Overplanting is a wasteful row gardening practice that we're trying to avoid, so seed planting and spacing is enormously important in SFG, even though it's pretty simple. Depending on how old the students are, a neat way to memorize the four different numbers of spacing is to ask what number sequence is 1-4-9-16? The answer is—Do you know?—Can you guess? Okay, I'll tell you. It is the square of 1-2-3-4. That simple. So we say, "SFG is as simple as 1-2-3-4." They will remember that. Can you? Does everyone know how to get squares of numbers? Of course.

Flashcard-type placards can be a handy tool for training students on proper planting patterns for different types of crops.

cabbage

A PASSING GRADE

WHAT KIND OF THINGS DO I NEED TO KNOW TO BECOME A CERTIFIED SFG INSTRUCTOR?

There's actually a quiz you'll need to pass (which is pretty easy because we give the answers along the way in your training). Here it is if you want to get a sense of what you'll need to know.

1. What did the gardening experts tell Mel when he asked why we single-row gardening techniques?
2. Describe SFG in a short, concise sentence.
3. Based on information in the book, what is the main advantage of SFG?
4. Based on information in the book, what five things are reduced through SFG?
5. Based on information in the book, what three laborious things are eliminated from row gardening versus SFG?
6. Based on information in the book, to whom will SFG appeal?
7. Based on information in the book, which people will think SFG is too simple to work?
8. The *ALL NEW Square Foot Gardening* book describes 10 basics of SFG and how and why each is important. In your own words, identify and describe those 10 items here.
9. The book identifies the "five points of location." What are they and why are they important?
10. The book describes a typical 4 × 4 bed. How deep is this bed? Where is it in relation to your existing soil? How much of your existing soil do you use?
11. Identify the three ingredients in Mel's Mix and describe the purpose of each.
12. When making homemade compost, what are the four "Ms" that will speed up the process?
13. When purchasing bags of compost, what are the advantages to buying several types?

14. How does SFG help conserve peat moss—a nonrenewable resource?
15. What is vermiculite?
16. What size vermiculite should be used in the SFG? And why?
17. Where does one normally purchase vermiculite?
18. How many cubic feet are in one 4 × 4 SFG box?
19. Based on information in the book, how is it recommended that the ingredients of Mel's Mix be mixed?
20. Why is it important to completely moisten Mel's Mix after filling the SFG boxes before planting?
21. Why is it important to add a grid to the top of every SFG box?
22. What materials does Mel recommend be used to make the grids for boxes?
23. Plant spacing differs by crop. Identify the four spacing options recommended in the book.
24. In the book, Mel recommends the use of only three tools. What are they and what is each used for?
25. How is crop rotation "automatic" in SFG?
26. Describe why there are so few weeds in a SFG.
27. In the book, Mel describes a specific process of watering the plants in a SFG. Describe this process.
28. Describe the process of replanting a square in a SFG.
29. Describe vertical gardening and how it works in a SFG.
30. List some common crops grown on a vertical frame.
31. Ideally, which side of a box should a vertical frame be placed?
32. How can your garden be protected from cats and dogs?
33. Describe how to make protective dome supports from PVC pipe.
34. List the different types of coverings that can go over the dome supports and the protection provided.
35. How is SFG especially suited for wheelchair, stand-up, or sit-down gardening?

Continued

36. How can school-age children benefit from having a SFG as part of their curriculum?
37. When gardening in humanitarian settings, what is the main difference in the soil used when gardening in a third-world country compared to a developed country?
38. After learning, studying, and implementing SFG in your own yard, what have you experienced?
39. How can YOU best make the world a better place through the use of sharing SFG with others?
40. Are you ready now to become an ambassador of SFG and spread this simple, easy, no-work gardening method to all those in need? How are you going to do that?
41. How can the SFGF help you in those efforts?

RESOURCES

AMERICAN COMMUNITY GARDENING ASSOCIATION (ACGA)

The ACGA is a non-profit organization dedicated to promoting the growth of community gardens throughout North America—in Canada and the United States. They offer guidance, advice and tips on starting and maintaining a community garden, as well as other resources that can be found on their website.

communitygarden.org
info@communitygarden.org
877-275-2242

COOPERATIVE EXTENSION SYSTEM

A program under the United States Department of Agriculture's National Institute of Food and Agriculture, the Cooperative Extension System is a nationwide educational network of offices—including state, regional and local—staffed by experts trained to provide practical information about local growing habitats, plants, pests and general agricultural issues. Initially set up to serve home farms, the system now serves anyone with an interest in gardening or agriculture.

www.csrees.usda.gov/Extension
202-720-4423

INDEX